HIGHER AND STANDARD

BUSINESS AND MANAGEMENT

Revision Notes

For use with the International Baccalaureate Diploma Business and Management Programme

Dexter R Phillips, Ed.D

Trafford
PUBLISHING

Printed in Victoria, BC, Canada.

ISBN: 978-1-4251-7149-0

Our mission is to efficiently provide the world's finest, most comprehensive book publishing service, enabling every author to experience success. To find out how to publish your book, your way, and have it available worldwide, visit us online at www.trafford.com

Trafford rev. 12/16/09

North America & international
toll-free: 1 888 232 4444 (USA & Canada)
phone: 250 383 6864 ♦ fax: 812 355 4082

CONTENTS

Aim of this book

This book is specifically written for students pursuing *Higher* and *Standard Levels* in the *Business and Management* courses offered by the *International Baccalaureate Organisation (IBO)*; however, it can also serve as a useful source of reference for those who may be pursuing similar programmes.

How to use this book

This book is designed to be used as support material for your studies of IBO's Higher and Standard Levels Business and Management courses. More specifically, it should be used:

√ As a supplement to your current business and management text, notes and lectures

√ To focus on the specific learning outcomes associated with each unit of the Business and Management syllabus

√ As a reference material to prepare you for your exams.

The assessment objectives

Having followed the Business and Management course at HL or SL students, will be expected to:

1. Demonstrate knowledge and understanding of business terminology, concepts, principles and theories

2. Make business decisions by identifying the issue(s), selecting and interpreting data, applying appropriate tools and techniques and recommending suitable solutions

3. Analyse and evaluate business decisions using a variety of sources

4. Evaluate business strategies and/or practice showing evidence of critical thinking

5. Apply skills and knowledge learned in the subject to hypothetical and real business situations

6. Communicate business ideas and information effectively and accurately using appropriate formats and tools.

In addition to the above students at HL will be expected to:

7. Synthesise knowledge in order to develop a framework for business decision making.

From the Business and Management First Examination 2009 Diploma Programme Guide. © The International Baccalaureate Organisation, 2007

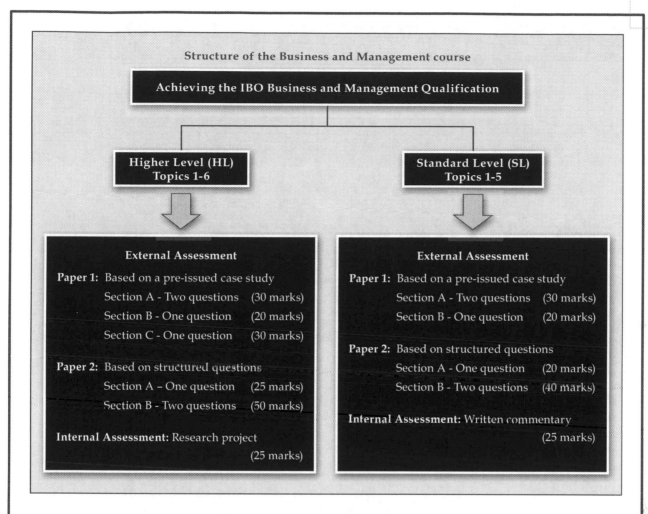

Structure of the Business and Management course

Achieving the IBO Business and Management Qualification

Higher Level (HL)
Topics 1-6

Standard Level (SL)
Topics 1-5

External Assessment

Paper 1: Based on a pre-issued case study

Section A - Two questions   (30 marks)

Section B - One question   (20 marks)

Section C - One question   (30 marks)

Paper 2: Based on structured questions

Section A – One question   (25 marks)

Section B - Two questions   (50 marks)

Internal Assessment: Research project

(25 marks)

External Assessment

Paper 1: Based on a pre-issued case study

Section A - Two questions   (30 marks)

Section B - One question   (20 marks)

Paper 2: Based on structured questions

Section A - One question   (20 marks)

Section B - Two questions   (40 marks)

Internal Assessment: Written commentary

(25 marks)

Your success in the Business and Management course

The Business and Management course is a rigorous two-year undertaking and your success depends on how well you:

√ Allocate your time to assigned readings and other related activities

√ Cope with and complete your Internal Assessment

√ Schedule and follow a revision routine

√ Engage your Business and Management teachers

√ Practise past-examination questions

√ Understand group-3 and subject-specific command terms*

√ Plan and manage your time in the exam.

* For a review of these terms, see *Glossary of command terms* on pages 74-75 of *The Business and Management syllabus.*

1.1: THE NATURE OF BUSINESS ACTIVITY

What is business?

Business is any commercial activity conducted with the objective of producing goods and/or services. While some business activities are performed for profit, others are not for profit.

Business inputs, outputs and processes

INPUTS	PROCESSES	OUTPUTS
Factors of production	Harvesting	**Goods and services**
Land: oil, timber, other raw materials	Banking and insurance	Food
Labour: people (skilled, semi-skilled)	Construction	Clothing
Capital: machine, building, money	Manufacturing	Entertainment
Enterprise: entrepreneur	**Value added at this stage**	Housing

Some other terms related to the nature of business activity

1. **Need:** A need can be described as a state of deprivation. It is the absence of basic goods and services that are necessary for our survival. For example, when we are hungry, we need food to satisfy our hunger.

2. **Want:** A want is a desire for specific satisfiers. For example, when we are hungry, any food will satisfy our hunger; however, our demand for a specific type of food translates into a want.

3. **Specialisation:** This refers to the separation of functions within a business. Each function is the responsibility of a specialist who has the appropriate knowledge and expertise to conduct the task effectively. For example, in a law firm, one partner may specialise in corporate law, while another may specialise in criminal law.

4. **Division of labour:** A job may be broken down into a number of tasks. Each task is carried out by an individual or a group of individuals designated for that role. For example, manufacturing a motor vehicle is broken down into many different tasks.

5. **Opportunity cost:** This refers to the alternative which must be given up in order to achieve something. For example, for a business, the opportunity cost of having a substantial amount of cash in the bank is the positive return on investment it would have earned if it had invested the money in a more profitable venture.

6. **Goods:** This refers to tangible items, such as furniture, clothing and cars. Goods can also be classified as consumer goods or capital goods.

7. **Service:** A service may be defined as a product with non-tangible attributes. For example, medical care, the services provided by a bank.

You must be able to **identify** inputs, outputs and processes of a business. © IBO, 2007

Business functions

All businesses irrespective of their size, conduct four (4) primary functions. In large businesses these functions are organised within specialised departments headed by managers or directors.

The **Marketing** function includes:

√ Generating market leads

√ Identifying target markets

√ Developing and implementing marketing plan

√ Selling, advertising and distribution.

The **Human Resources** function includes:

√ Recruitment, selection, training and evaluation

√ Dismissals and rewards

√ Employee welfare and remuneration

√ Negotiations with Trade Unions.

The **Production** function includes:

√ Production of goods

√ Quality control

√ Research and Development

√ Location decisions.

The **Finance** function includes:

√ Financial monitoring and control

√ Financial record-keeping

√ Budget coordination

√ Receipts and payments.

You must be able to:

1. **Describe** how business activity combines human, physical and financial resources to create goods and services.

2. **Explain** the role of different business departments in overall business activity.

© IBO, 2007

Primary, secondary and tertiary sectors

Sector	Explanation	Examples of business activities
Primary	The activities in this sector are associated with the **extraction of raw materials** (natural resources).	Fishing, mining, logging and harvesting.
Secondary	**Manufacturing** is the physical or chemical transformation of raw materials into finished products.	Manufacturing of furniture, packaged food, and clothing.
Secondary	**Construction** refers to planning, building and managing structures.	Construction of roads, factories and offices.
Tertiary	This sector is concerned with the provision of **services**.	Banking, insurance, education, transportation, health and entertainment.

You must be able to **explain** the nature of business activities in each sector.   © The IBO, 2007

Changes in economic structure: Impact on business activity
(HIGHER LEVEL FOCUS)

A change in economic structure is represented by a shift in the level of output and employment between the primary, secondary and tertiary sectors. The relative importance of each sector is based on the **value of goods** and **services produced** and the **number of people employed**.

Changes in economic structure can impact business activity in the following ways:

√ Decline in the availability of workers, as labour shifts from one sector to another

√ Increase in wage rates in some sectors

√ Adaptation or adjustment to new government legislation, e.g., taxation policies

√ Increased spending on professional development, communication and technology

√ Economies of scale as the secondary and tertiary sectors allow for substantial growth in business activities.

You must be able to **analyse** the impact of changes in economic structure on business activity. © The IBO, 2007

1.2: TYPES OF ORGANISATION

Private sector

The private sector comprises privately owned businesses, e.g., private and public companies.

Objectives of the private sector

The following are some objectives of organisations in the private sector:

√ Increase market share

√ Increase sales

√ Maximise profit

√ Gain market dominance

√ Fulfill Corporate Social Responsibilities.

Public sector

The public sector comprises organisations which are administered by the government, e.g., post offices, public hospitals and public schools.

Objectives of the public sector

The following are some objectives of organisations in the public sector:

√ Provide and maintain public goods and services

√ Ensure economic stability

√ Reduce unemployment.

You must be able to **distinguish** between the organisations in private and public sectors. © The IBO, 2007

The relationship between organisations in private and public sectors
(HIGHER LEVEL FOCUS)

The relationship between private and public sectors

One of the main characteristics of mixed economies is that they have clearly defined public and private sectors. Although these two sectors have different objectives, they are interdependent.

(Contd...)

The relationship between private and public sectors takes many forms and includes various activities:

√ Cooperation on public-works projects, such as construction of roads, sea defences, tunnels and schools

√ The private sector's payment of taxes to the government provides main source of national revenue

√ Partnerships between Non-Governmental Organisations and government agencies to provide aid and funding for crucial development projects

√ Partnerships on national development and investment strategies

√ Collaboration on medical projects (for example, the development and distribution of vital vaccination and other required medical facilities to poor communities).

You must be able to **analyse** the relationship between organisations in private and public sectors.

© The IBO, 2007

Starting a business
Reasons for setting up a business

√ Achieve independence, self-reliance and job security

√ Pursue an interest or a hobby

√ Make money

√ Expand an existing business

√ Provide goods and/or services

√ Achieve self-employment, after being retrenched/laid off from a job

You must be able to **explain** the reasons for starting a business.   © The IBO, 2007

The process of starting a business

The entrepreneur generates the business idea, seeks out and identifies market opportunities and appropriate funding, combines the factors of production, decides to go ahead with investing in the business venture and assumes all the risks associated with such decision.

Some important considerations for starting a business

√ Business idea and identification of market opportunities

√ Business plan

√ Sources of funding

√ Government business legislation and how it may impact the business

√ Goods and/or services to be offered

√ Source and skills of employees

√ Market segment to be served

√ Location of the business premises

√ Potential suppliers

√ Availability of fixed assets

You must be able to **explain** the process of setting up a business.   © The IBO, 2007

Possible problems faced by business start-ups

√ Lack of funding

√ Inexperienced managers

√ Poor location

√ Poor market research

√ Inadequate cash flow

√ Inability to penetrate target market

√ Difficult economic conditions

√ High production costs

You must be able to **analyse** the problems that business start-ups may face.   © The IBO, 2007

Profit-based organisations

Sole trader: A business owned and managed by one person,
e.g., the vendor who sells ice-cream on the street.

Advantages	Disadvantages
√ Easy to establish, with very few legal formalities	√ Unlimited liability: Sole traders are liable for debts beyond their investment
√ Owner enjoys all the profit	√ Limited sources of funding
√ Good rapport and close relationship with customers	√ No continuity: The death of the owner marks the death of the business
√ Freedom to choose how the business is managed	√ Inability to benefit from economies of scale.
√ Quick decision making.	

Partnership: Two or more (fewer than 20) individuals come together in business,
with the aim of making profits.

Advantages	Disadvantages
√ A wider capital base for the business	√ Unlimited liability
√ Shared workload, based on skills and competencies	√ Decision making requires consultation and may be time-consuming
√ Shared decision making and responsibility	√ All partners bound by the actions of one
√ Few legal formalities required for start-up	√ Profits shared
√ Privacy of financial affairs	√ No continuity - the partnership is dissolved if one partner opts out of the business.
√ Partners are legally bound by a deed of partnership.	

NOTE: A deed of partnership is a legal agreement which governs the affairs of the partners.

Some specifications addressed in a partnership deed are:

- √ Capital investment by each partner
- √ Model for sharing profit or loss
- √ Responsibility of each partner
- √ Procedure for inducting new partner (s)
- √ Procedure for dissolution of the partnership.

Companies/Corporations

A company is a legal entity which is owned by a group of people who are referred to as shareholders – people who have acquired shares/stocks in the company.

Main characteristics of companies

- √ Limited liability
- √ Separate legal identity
- √ Clear distinction between ownership and control
- √ Continuity
- √ Ownership by shareholders
- √ Capital can be raised through sale of shares
- √ Board of Directors controls the activities of a company on behalf of its shareholders.

Companies can be classified as either Private Limited Companies (Ltd) or Public Limited Companies (Plc)

Characteristics of private limited companies

- √ Restrictions on raising capital: General public are not allowed to buy shares
- √ Usually, shares are owned by family members and close associates
- √ Name ends with *Ltd*.
- √ Shares cannot be transferred without the approval of directors
- √ Usually, small-to-medium-size businesses

Characteristics of public limited companies

- √ Name ends with *Plc*.
- √ Board of Directors controls the company
- √ Quoted on the stock exchange
- √ Most capital raised through sale of shares
- √ Shares sold to the general public
- √ Usually, very large entities/businesses

Advantages of companies

Limited companies benefit from the following factors:

- √ Separate legal identity
- √ Continuity
- √ Limited liability
- √ Substantial capital raised from shares
- √ Economies of scale
- √ Diverse range of human-resource expertise.

Disadvantages of companies

Limited companies are constrained by the following factors:

- √ Diseconomies of scale
- √ High set-up cost
- √ Lack of financial privacy (Yearly audit)
- √ Risk of takeover
- √ Bureaucracy in formation.

How companies are formed

| Memorandum of Association + Article of Association |

Outlines issues relating to the external affairs of the company	Outlines how the company's internal affairs will be governed
√ Name of the company. √ Address of registered office. √ Objectives of the company. √ Capital to be raised. √ Value of shares.	√ Procedures for transfer of shares. √ Powers and conduct of directors. √ Voting rights of members. √ Procedure for general meetings.

Certificate of Incorporation
A document which allows the company to begin operations

Company formed
Private or Public Limited Company

Floatation
The company listed on the stock exchange (Public Limited Company)

Summary of business organisations and their main characteristics

Type of business organisation	Main characteristics
Sole Trader	√ Responsible for all business affairs √ Unlimited liability √ Keeps entire profits, bears all losses
Partnership	√ Shared capital investment and control √ Unlimited liability √ Shared profits or losses √ Co-ownership of property
Companies/Corporations	√ Limited liability √ Separate legal identity √ Continuity

You must be able to **distinguish** between different types of business organisations and **identify** their main characteristics.

The extent to which ownership and control differ in organisations is determined by a number of factors:

√ Size of the organisation

√ Availability of or access to funding

√ Management/owner's corporate objectives

√ Influence of investors and other stakeholders

√ Government's business and investment policies.

You must be able to **analyse** the extent to which ownership and control differ in organisations. © The IBO, 2007

The most appropriate form of ownership for a firm is determined by several factors:

√ Size of the firm

√ Corporate objectives

√ Need for limited or unlimited liability

√ Availability of funding

√ Nature of activities which the firm intends to carry out

√ Extent to which owners want to relinquish or maintain control of the firm.

You must be able to **evaluate** the most appropriate form of ownership for a firm. © The IBO, 2007

The division between ownership and control

Organisation	Ownership	Control
Sole Trader	Owner/Sole Trader	Owner/Sole Trader
Partnership	Partners	Partners
Private Limited Company	Shareholders: family and close associates	Directors, on behalf of shareholders
Public Limited Company	Shareholders: general public	Directors, on behalf of shareholders

---

Division between ownership and control: The impact on stakeholders

Sole trader: The impact of division between ownership and control on stakeholders

Owner

√ Complete control over activities and decisions

√ Quick decision making, as no approvals have to be sought from internal stakeholders

√ Close relationship with employees and customers

√ No economies of scale

(Contd...)

Employees

√ Closely supervised

√ Direct communication with owner strengthens employer-employee relationship

√ Benefit from delegation of key functions, for e.g., the owner of a small shop might ask an employee to operate the shop in her absence

Competitors

√ Easier to understand the nature of the sole trader's operations (products and services)

√ Due to the private nature of sole trader's business, competitors may find it difficult to access information about its activities

Suppliers

√ Often develop a one-to-one business relationship with the sole trader

√ Relationship is less stable as the sole trader is exposed to the risk of going out of business

√ Do not have to offer huge discounts/rebates as the sole trader's volume of purchase is generally low

Special interest groups

√ Relatively easy to monitor the developments in the business

---

Partnership: The impact of division between ownership and control on stakeholders

Owners

√ Shared expertise and decision making

√ Shared workload, profits and losses

√ The action of one affects all

√ Unlimited liability status makes owners vulnerable to personal losses if the business fails

Employees

√ Access to owners simplifies the communication process

√ Do not have to deal with bureaucracy associated with larger organisations

√ Opportunities for becoming a partner may be limited or non-existent

Customers

√ Enjoy personalised services

√ Benefit from personal access to partners

√ Do not have a say in who controls the partnership

(Contd...)

Competitors

√ Due to the private nature of partnerships, competitors may find it difficult to access information about their activities

√ Opportunities for collaboration on projects/business ventures of mutual interest

Suppliers

√ Closer alignment with partnership businesses

√ Less sensitive to the likelihood that the partnership may go out of business

√ Willing to offer favourable credit terms as more than one individual is accountable for the firm's debts

Special interest groups

√ Relatively easy to monitor the actions of the firm

Limited companies: The impact of division between ownership and control on stakeholders

Shareholders

√ Limited liability status

√ Limited say in how the company is controlled – restricted to a vote at the company's Annual General Meeting (AGM)

√ Right to transfer ownership of shares is restricted to the company's directors – private limited companies

√ No restrictions on the right to transfer ownership of shares – public limited companies

√ No say in how the activities of the company are managed on a day-to-day basis

Managers

√ Control operational aspects of a company, on behalf of the shareholders

√ Actions are limited by their responsibility to the directors and shareholders of the company

√ Opportunities for promotion

Employees

√ Restricted by bureaucracy of decision making

√ May benefit from the company's strong corporate image

√ Benefit by being delegated various functions and responsibilities which enhance experience and expertise

√ Must follow protocols and designated communication channels while communicating information to management

√ No direct access to directors of the company

√ Many opportunities for promotion within the company

(Cont.)

Customers

√ May benefit from variety of goods and services

√ Customer complaints may not be dealt with promptly – because of bureaucratic structure

√ Opportunity to be part owners of public limited companies

Competitors

√ Access to financial and other data of public limited companies as these are made available to the public – full disclosure

√ May be limited by the information they can access about the financial position of private limited companies

√ Can buy into public limited companies

√ May be in a strong position to merge with or take over a weak company

Suppliers

√ Suppliers are often required to extend favourable credit terms, due to the size and influence of companies

√ Risk of being taken over by companies to which they supply components, raw materials or services

√ Can purchase shares in public limited companies

The government

√ Legislation on competitive practice of companies

√ Corporate taxes

√ Consumer protection

√ Regulation of activities of companies

You must be able to **analyse** the impact of the division between ownership and control on internal and external stakeholders.

© The IBO, 2007

Non-profit and non-governmental organisations

Non-profit organisations

Non-profit organisations: Organisations whose activities are not tied to the pursuit of profit. Peter Drucker describes non-profit organisations as entities which are led by their values rather than financial commitment to their stakeholders.

NOTE: It is acceptable for non-profit organisations to generate surplus from the services they provide. This surplus is then reinvested into sustaining and developing the organisation. For example, schools which operate as non-profit entities use the surplus generated from fees to invest in new and existing facilities and programmes.

Non-Governmental Organisations (NGOs)

Non-governmental organisations: These entities are independent of the direct control of government. The objectives of NGOs are social in nature and geared towards enhancing the wellbeing of communities. General examples of NGOs are **charities** and **pressure groups**.

√ Charities (e.g., The Red Cross, Salvation Army, the Global Fund for Children)

√ Foundations (e.g., The Ford Foundation, The International Youth Foundation)

√ Pressure/Advocacy groups (e.g., Amnesty International, Trade Unions)

NOTE: Non-governmental organisations serve various causes; hence, each organisation works towards achieving objectives which are specific to its cause.

Charities: Organisations which exist for the sole purpose of helping the underprivileged. They are mainly financed through fund-rising activities and monetary donations from businesses and individuals. Charities are regarded as non-profit entities.

Advantages

√ Charities enjoy tax exemptions.

√ Corporate and individual donors can sometimes avail tax benefits/exemptions on the donations made to charities.

√ Charities have a very good chance of securing donations from government and other similar organisations.

Disadvantages

√ Compliance with stringent rules and regulations governing their operations

√ Lack of financial incentives for employees

√ Limited sources of funding

√ Restricted by their charitable objectives

Pressure groups: Organisations of people who believe in the same cause and seek to influence governmental and organisational policies to back their cause. They may strive to change the attitude of organisations or governments towards environment, workers, consumers, citizens, or nations.

Advantages

√ Pressure groups may work for the general good of the public and persuade corporations to alter/shun business activities which have a negative impact on society.

√ Businesses and governments are made accountable for their social and corporate actions.

√ Public awareness of government and business activities and their effects is heightened.

Disadvantages

√ Pressure groups are often regarded as disturbers of economic progress and peace.

√ Some pressure groups use violence as a method of gaining attention for their cause.

Examples of international pressure groups

√ Amnesty International

√ Greenpeace International

√ Trade Unions

You must be able to **compare** and **contrast** the objectives of NGOs, non-profit organisations and other organisations.

© The IBO, 2007

The impact of the actions of NGOs and other non-profit organisations is determined by:

√ Their objectives

√ Their financial strength

√ Their influence within the government

√ Their popularity

√ Their level of organisation

√ Their ability to mobilise public support

You must be able to **analyse** the impact of the actions of NGOs and other non-profit organisations.

© The IBO 2007

Public-private enterprise
(HIGHER LEVEL FOCUS)

The nature of public-private partnerships

Public-private enterprise refers to the collaboration between businesses from private sector and the government to provide community facilities, infrastructure or services.

You must be able to **explain** the nature of public-private partnership.   © The IBO, 2007

Costs and benefits of public-private partnerships

Costs	Benefits
√ Reduction in government control over key resources, manufacturing and services	√ Improved service delivery
√ Inability to respond to changing public demands	√ Improved cost-effectiveness
√ Financial risk for government	√ Increased investment in public infrastructure
√ Increase in the cost of goods and services to the public	√ Reduced public-sector risks
√ Self-interest of private sector	√ Lower unemployment rate
	√ Economic development

You must be able to **analyse** the costs and benefits of cooperation between public and private sectors.

© The IBO, 2007

1.3: ORGANISATIONAL OBJECTIVES

Organisational objectives are the goals a business seeks to achieve.

The importance of objectives in managing an organisation

Objectives

√ Help organisations to precisely identify what they want to achieve.

√ Provide a means by which management can quantify goals and evaluate performance.

√ Serve as a control mechanism.

√ Provide a sense of purpose, focus, direction and motivation for management and employees.

√ Serve as the starting point for the development and implementation of business strategies.

√ Clarify the goals of organisation for all stakeholders.

You must be able to **explain** the importance of objectives in managing an organisation.

© The IBO, 2007

The need to change objectives
(HIGHER LEVEL FOCUS)

A number of internal and external factors may influence an organisation to change its objectives over time.

Internal factors	External factors
√ Change in size and structure of the business	√ Changes in government policy
√ Change in corporate culture	√ Competition
√ Location or re-location	√ Economic factors
√ Availability of finance	√ Changing state of technology
√ Interest of stakeholders	√ Expectation of external stakeholders (e.g.,customers)
√ Internal stakeholders' attitude towards change	√ Demographic changes

You must be able to **evaluate** the need for organisations to change objectives in response to changes in internal and external environments.

© IBO, 2007

Statements

Mission and vision statements

Mission statement: A clear and concise statement that spells out an organisation's purpose for existence.

Vision statement: A description of where or what the organisation aspires to be. A vision statement *paints* the ideal future.

Difference between mission and vision statements

Mission statements give internal and external stakeholders a sense of what the organisation strives to achieve.

Vision statements are forward-looking and futuristic in nature.

The purpose/role of mission and vision statements

An organisation's mission statement stems out of its vision statement. Vision and mission statements are interrelated and serve the following purposes:

√ Outline the measures for success

√ Shape the values of the organisation

√ Influence management and employees behaviour

√ Outline the road map for the organisation

√ Provide external stakeholders with useful insights into the organisation

√ Create a sense of desire and commitment from management and employees.

You must be able to:

1. **Explain** the purpose of mission and vision statements.
2. **Analyse** the role of mission and vision statements in an organisation.

© The IBO, 2007

Aims and objectives

Aims

Aims are the long–term, far-reaching goals of the business. They are broad statements of purpose indicating how the business would like to be positioned in the industry in relation to its competitors.

Although corporate aims are vague and cannot be measured against specific outcomes, they assume importance because of the following reasons:

√ Enable development of more specific, measurable goals (corporate objectives)

√ Serve as sources of motivation for management and employees

√ Serve as bases upon which organisational plans can be developed and implemented.

Objectives

Objectives are the more specific and precise goals an organisation seeks to achieve. They are developed from corporate aims.

Objectives are **SMART**

SPECIFIC: Must state exactly what the company intends to achieve.

MEASURABLE: Must be quantifiable.

ACHIEVABLE: Must be attainable.

REALISTIC: Must reflect goals which can be achieved with available resources.

TIME: Must be attainable in a realistic timeframe.

Objectives must also be **appropriate**. That is, they must be **consistent** with the mission and vision of the organisation. In addition, objectives must be **agreed** upon, must **reflect consensus** and must be **communicated** to all members of the organisation.

Strategic objectives and tactical/operational objectives

Strategy

A strategy is a plan of action which is developed and implemented to accomplish a goal. It is the *road map* of how the firm will achieve its objectives.

Strategic objectives

Strategic objectives are well-defined long-term goals. They are mainly concerned with establishing the organisation's position in the future and are determined at the highest level of management. Strategic objectives can relate to outcomes such as:

√ Market share   √ Expansion and growth

√ Infrastructure   √ International expansion

√ Profit maximisation   √ Corporate culture development

Operational/tactical objectives

Operational/tactical objectives are short-term goals which are designed to support an organisation's broader strategic objectives. For example, to support a strategic objective of increasing market share by 20% in 2009, the marketing department may devise an operational objective to increase the size of the sales team.

The relationship between aims, objectives, strategies and tactics

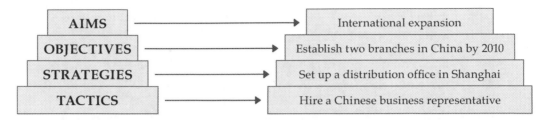

AIMS	→	International expansion
OBJECTIVES	→	Establish two branches in China by 2010
STRATEGIES	→	Set up a distribution office in Shanghai
TACTICS	→	Hire a Chinese business representative

Some additional notes on strategy

To achieve its corporate objectives, a business can develop and implement a variety of strategies:

Corporate strategies: Long-term plans to achieve an organisation's corporate objectives (e.g., a decision to merge with another company).

Generic strategies: Strategic options that can be used to gain sustainable competitive advantage (e.g., **differentiation strategies, cost-leadership strategies** and **focus strategies**).

Functional strategies: Specific plans for improving the efficiency of departments and other business units (e.g., professional-development training for employees in the finance department).

Global strategies: Specific plans for entering international markets (e.g., McDonalds has established a significant presence in China through a number of franchises).

Ethical objectives

Business ethics

Business ethics are the values and principles businesses adhere to in their dealings with stakeholders. Some examples of ethical strategies and behaviour are:

1. Fair pricing of products and services

2. Policies and actions to reduce pollution

3. Fair wages

4. Contribution towards community development.

Ethical objectives are the goals which are in line with an organisation's values and principles. For many organisations, these values and principles are outlined in their standard ethical code of practice.

The following are some reasons why organisations set ethical objectives:

√ To comply with industry standards and regulations

√ To benefit from government incentives which are given to organisations that exemplify good ethical practices within their respective industries

√ To establish or maintain credible corporate image

√ To fulfill their Corporate Social Responsibility.

You must be able to **explain** the reasons why organisations consider setting ethical objectives. © The IBO, 2007

Advantages of ethical objectives

√ Enhance an organisation's credibility and corporate image

√ Help attract ethical investors, customers, employees and suppliers

√ Boost staff morale and motivation

√ Maximise shareholders' value

Disadvantages of ethical objectives

√ Increase in operational costs

√ Conflict among stakeholders

√ Focus on maximising returns for shareholders is lessened

√ Ethical initiatives are not always appreciated

You must be able to:

1. **Analyse** the advantages and disadvantages of ethical objectives.

2. **Discuss** the impact of implementing ethical objectives.

© The IBO, 2007

Corporate Social Responsibility (CSR)

Corporate Social Responsibility (CSR) is about business organisations taking account of the social, environmental and economic impact of their activities on stakeholders and the wider society.

What drives an organisation to be socially responsible?

√ Competition

√ Government legislation

√ Corporate culture

√ Consumers' sensitivity and awareness

√ Pressure groups

Different views of Corporate Social Responsibility

Some views on social responsibility in an international context

√ Corporate Social Responsibility initiatives do not benefit the business. They distract directors, managers and workers from focusing on maximising profits and shareholder values.

√ Companies engage in Corporate Social Responsibility initiatives to avoid being pressured by narrow interest groups. It is about maintaining a good public image.

√ Businesses and the communities in which they operate are in sustainable partnerships; it is natural for businesses to care.

√ When Corporate Social Responsibility initiatives are linked to specific operational goals, both the business and the society will reap tangible benefits.

√ Corporate Social Responsibility creates shared values for both the business and the society.

Some policies to implement objectives of Corporate Social Responsibility

√ Non-discriminatory hiring and promotion policies

√ Responsible waste-management

√ Effective use and management of resources (for example, using recycled paper)

√ Fair trading practices

√ Environmental auditing

√ Sourcing ethical, socially responsible suppliers

You must be able to **explain** the different views that organisations may have of their social responsibility, in an international context.

© The IBO, 2007

Social and environmental auditing

Social audit: An activity that allows organisations to examine and assess the impact of their economic and social activities on the community in which they operate.

Environmental audit: A process through which organisations examine the impact of their economic activities on the immediate environment in which they operate.

Value of social and environmental audits

√ The audits indicate the extent to which organisations meet their social and environmental objectives.

√ The results of these audits can help enhance an organisation's Corporate–Social-Responsibility initiatives, e.g., a decision to use recyclable packaging for its products.

√ The results of these audits can help organisations improve their accountability to stakeholders.

√ The audits can be used by organisations to advocate and reaffirm their commitment to socially responsible and environmentally friendly policies.

Limitations of social and environmental audits

√ Carrying out these audits is an expensive and time-consuming affair.

√ Organisations may not have the time or resources to implement recommendations resulting from the audits.

The value of social and environmental audits to different stakeholders

Employees

√ Understand the impact of the organisation's Corporate Social Responsibility initiatives within national and international contexts

√ Understand the impact of the organisation's activities on the environment

√ Are motivated to work for an organisation whose strong corporate image reflects the positive outcomes of its social and environmental audits.

Shareholders

√ Relate to the nature of the company and the extent of its contribution to the community

√ Understand the impact of the organisation's activities on the environment

√ May be keen on investing in companies with an outstanding record of social and environmental responsibility

√ Use the audit results to calculate the cost associated with Corporate Social Responsibility initiatives taken up by the company.

Managers

√ Understand the impact of the organisation's activities on the environment

√ Use the audit results in the strategic-planning process

√ Use the audit results to identify weaknesses in the implementation of their Corporate Social Responsibility policies.

Customers

√ Support businesses which exhibit social and environmental responsibility

√ Learn about the social and environmental initiatives taken up by the businesses they support.

Suppliers

√ Ethical suppliers will not engage with businesses whose corporate images are tarnished by poor social and environmental records.

√ Use the audit results to confirm that they are dealing with responsible partners

√ Use the audit results to assess whether the businesses to which they supply goods or services are in line with their own corporate principles.

The government

√ The audit results help the government determine the extent to which businesses comply with regulations governing social and environmental responsibilities.

√ Unfavourable results drive the government towards legislating and enforcing regulations aimed at protecting the stakeholders and the environment.

√ Some governments use the audit results to identify and reward companies for their responsible behaviour.

Special interest organisations

√ Special interest organisations, use the results from social and environmental audits to monitor the actions of businesses.

You must be able to **analyse** the value of social and environmental audits to different stakeholders.

© The IBO, 2007

Changes in Corporate Social Responsibility over time
(HIGHER LEVEL FOCUS)

As the internal and external environments in which a firm operates change, so does the firm's view of its social responsibility changes accordingly. The following are some reasons why a firm's view of its social responsibility:

√ Changes in corporate objectives

√ Changes in corporate culture

√ Availability of funding for CSR initiatives

√ Impact of pressure-group influence on the firm's operations

√ Changes in society's attitudes towards the firm's products or services.

√ State of the economy

√ Expectations of stakeholders

√ Changes in government legislation

You must be able to **discuss** why a firm's views of its social responsibilities may change over time.

© The IBO, 2007

Change in attitude towards social responsibility
(HIGHER LEVEL FOCUS)

Why do firms' attitudes towards social responsibility change over time?

√ The extent to which firms are given government incentives may change.

√ A new board of directors or management team may have a different view of the extent to which the organisation should be socially responsible.

√ The geographic location of a business in developing or developed countries affects its attitudes towards social-responsibility initiatives.

√ The power of pressure groups and the impact of their actions can influence the behaviour of firms.

Why do societies' attitudes towards social responsibility change over time?

√ People are becoming increasingly aware that firms have a moral obligation to be socially responsible.

√ Societies view the socially responsible initiatives of firms as important to the development of their communities.

√ With changes in norms and values, people's views and expectations regarding the behaviour of businesses change.

You must be able to **discuss** why attitudes towards social responsibility may change over time.

© The IBO, 2007

Changes in societal norms and the behaviour of firms
(HIGHER LEVEL FOCUS)

Impact of changes in societal norms on the behaviour of firms

Societal norms are the values, beliefs, attitudes and behaviour of a group of people. Changes in societal norms affect the behaviour of firms in the following manner:

√ Change corporate objectives

√ Become more environment-friendly

√ Improve their commitments to being equal-opportunity employers

√ Become more conscious of their responsibility towards the community in which they operate

√ Adopt more ethical practices while dealing with stakeholders, such as suppliers and competitors

√ Strive to achieve national and international quality standards.

You must be able to **analyse** the impact of changes in societal norms on the way firms behave in a national and international context.

© The IBO, 2007

Why firms choose different strategies towards their social responsibilities

Factors influencing the choice of strategies for fulfilling social responsibilities

√ Competition

√ State of the economy

√ Values and beliefs of management

√ Nature of the business in which the firm is engaged

√ Geographical location (urban or rural area, local or international)

You must be able to **analyse** why firms choose different strategies towards their social responsibilities.

© The IBO, 2007

1.4: STAKEHOLDERS: INTERNAL AND EXTERNAL

> Stakeholders are those individuals and organisations with a vested interest in the firm and its activities.

Internal stakeholders and their interests

Stakeholders	Interest
Employees	√ Fair and reasonable remuneration for their work √ Health and safety at work √ Adequate retirement benefits
Shareholders	√ Capital gains – increasing returns on investment √ Payment of dividends √ Status of the company, at domestic and international levels
Manager	√ Development and maintenance of status and power √ Autonomy to execute planned goals √ Profit and organisational growth √ Formulation and implementation of appropriate strategies

External stakeholders and their interests

Stakeholders	Interest
Suppliers	√ Timely payment √ Maintenance of reputation with profitable firm √ Performance and corporate image
Customers	√ Quality goods and service √ Fair prices for the goods and services they buy √ CSR initiatives of the firm
Competitors	√ Market share, sales revenue, profitability √ Business strategies √ Research-and-Development focus
Special interest groups, e.g., Trade Unions	√ Employment benefits √ Employees' rights and protection √ Health-and-safety programmes and procedures √ Training and development of employees

You must be able to **explain** the interests of internal and external stakeholders. © The IBO, 2007

Stakeholder conflict

Conflict arises because the objectives and expectations of stakeholders are often very different. For example, shareholders' objectives may be to have management concentrate less on social projects, while management may view such projects as vital to the long term profitability and corporate image of the firm.

Some possible areas of conflict between stakeholders

√ Employee pay and benefits, e.g., issues of employees' health and safety while they are on the job

√ Shareholders seeking annual dividend payments and maximum returns on their investments

√ Managers' decision to reinvest profits in expansion projects rather than paying out dividends

√ Managers' and shareholders' views on ethical behaviour and social responsibility

Possible ways to overcome stakeholder conflict
(HIGHER LEVEL FOCUS)

1. **Negotiation:** The stakeholders involved in a conflict soften their stands and agree to a compromise on their positions (e.g., settlement of dispute between employees and management).

2. **Mediation:** A third party facilitates the process of negotiations between stakeholders who cannot find a common solution to their conflict.

3. **Accommodation:** Stakeholders, who may be in a position of power, satisfy the objectives of other stakeholders while overlooking some elements of their own objectives. For example, to accommodate the concern of an environmental group, an oil company suspends its offshore drilling activities.

4. **Compromise:** Stakeholders set aside their views and work towards a mutually favourable solution.

5. **Collaboration:** Different stakeholder groups are actively involved in finding the best solution to the conflict (e.g., management and employee's representatives collaborate on the development and implementation of a health-care plan for employees).

NOTE: Firms can never meet all the objectives of their stakeholders, so conflicts will arise; however, conflicts can be minimised if managers understand the key stakeholders and the extent to which meeting or not meeting their objectives affects business activities.

1.5: EXTERNAL ENVIRONMENT

The external environment refers to the forces which are outside of the firm and significantly influence its operations. These forces are referred to as **PEST** elements: **Political, Economic, Sociological** and **Technological**.

Other elements of the external environment include **Legal** and **Environmental** considerations, and hence, the acronym **PESTLE**.

PEST analysis

PEST analysis is an audit of the external-environment elements which may have a positive or negative impact on a firm's objectives and strategies.

A PEST framework

POLITICAL

Political stability, government corruption or instability, government policies, type of government, likely political change, legislations

ECONOMIC

Level of economic growth and development, inflation, exchange rates, interest rates, unemployment, globalisation

SOCIAL/CULTURAL

Changing social norms, demographic changes, changing lifestyles and attitudes, communication barriers, education, social barriers, attitude towards work

TECHNOLOGICAL

Changing communication technology and cost, technological advances in machinery and production systems, research and development

The process involved in conducting a PEST analysis

1. **Brainstorm** all factors that are relevant to the business environment.

2. **Identify** the information that is associated with these factors (e.g., interest rates apply to the economic factor).

3. **Draw** conclusions about how the factors can affect present and future policies and decisions.

You must be able to:

1. **Prepare** a PEST analysis from a given situation.

2. **Conduct** a PEST analysis to **analyse** the impact of the external environment on a firm.

Change in any of the PEST/PESTLE factors: Examples of possible impact on a firm's objectives and strategy

Example for change in PEST/PESTLE factors	Impact on firm's objectives	Impact on strategy
Political: Stringent government regulation on carbon emissions	The firm may decide to drastically reduce its carbon emissions within a short timeframe.	The firm may decide to use alternative sources of energy.
Economic: Increase in demand for a firm's product or service	The firm may decide to increase its market share by a higher percentage.	The firm shifts its focus from market-consolidation strategies to market-expansion strategies.
Social/Cultural: People become more environment-friendly	The firm may have to review its objectives with regard to the establishment of a recycling policy.	The firm decides to use recyclable materials for packaging its products.
Technological: Changes in communication technology	The firm may focus on upgrading its communication infrastructure within a shorter timeframe.	The firm allocates more funds for upgrading its existing infrastructure.

You must be able to **evaluate** the impact of a change in any of the PEST/PESTLE factors on a firm's objectives and strategy.

© The IBO, 2007

Opportunities and threats: STEEPLE factors

External environmental elements	Some examples of opportunities	Some examples of threats
Social/Cultural factors		
Changing social norms Demographic changes Lifestyles Attitudes towards foreign products Language	Product differentiation Diversification Research and development Increased revenue from sales Labour supply: Educated workforce Cultural integration	Increase in operating costs Mobility of labour Competition Outdated products or services
Technological factors		
Global communications E-commerce Innovation Automation and mechanisation	Improvement in production process Efficiency in operation Ease of communication New-product development Technology sharing/transfer Increase in employment	Increase in costs Stakeholder resentment Negative publicity Need for a highly skilled workforce

External environmental elements	Some examples of opportunities	Some examples of threats
Economic factors		
Economic growth Inflation Interest rates Exchange rate Unemployment	Increase in demand for goods and services Increase in value of fixed assets Increase in prices, increase in sales revenue, better leverage on import of raw materials The availability of a larger pool of labour	Competition Increase in wage bill Reduction in customer spending Rising costs for exporters Drop in demand Drop in the value of debtors
Environmental factors		
Climate change - good or poor weather conditions Global warming Ecological issues Environmental legislation	Enhanced corporate image Employing green technology Community outreach Recycling	Limits production, e.g., bad harvest Costly Conflict with pressure groups Stringent environmental legislation
Political factors		
Government policies Political stability Government corruption	Incentives for investment Lower operational costs Confidence in the economy	Unstable governments Stringent business legislations Bureaucracy
Legal		
Consumer legislation Employment legislation Anti-competitive practice laws	Revision of quality-control standards Implementation of quality-control standards Commitment from employees and customers Fair trading across the industry	Increase in costs Stricter regulations and inspections Likelihood of lawsuits
Ethical		
Fair trading practices Fair treatment of employees Contribution to community development	Excellent image and reputation Increase in sales Market dominance Stronger corporate brand	Other stakeholders and management conflict Increase in costs Loss of corporate focus

You must be able to:

1. **Analyse** the impact that external opportunities and threats may have on business objectives and strategies.

2. **Explain** how external opportunities and threats can impact decision making and SWOT (Strengths, Weaknesses, Opportunities, threats) analysis.

1.6: ORGANISATIONAL PLANNING TOOLS

The business plan

Business start-ups need effective plans, especially those which seek external funding. Based on the business plan, financial institutions assess the cost and risk associated with financing a business idea.

The business plan, therefore, is a document which gives financial institutions or potential investors a clear view of the nature of the proposed business venture, the strategies which will be employed to make it successful, the profitability of the business venture, and its potential for paying back the capital invested.

Elements of a business plan

Executive summary: Provides a clear and succinct overview of what is covered in the business plan.

Business: Gives a general description of the nature and legal structure of the proposed or existing business. It includes elements, such as the physical address and legal status of the business, nature of products or services offered, and factors that will make the business successful.

Market analysis: Provides comprehensive analysis of competitors, description of the industry, market trends, and nature of the market segment to be targeted.

Marketing strategies: Details the strategies to be employed to successfully market the firm's products or services.

Human resources: Presents the qualification and experience of the management team and other individuals who are deemed critical to the success of the business venture.

Financial analysis: Details cash-flow forecasts, break-even analysis, amount of capital needed and repayment options.

You must be able to:

1. **Analyse** the importance of the information in the business plan to different stakeholders.

2. **Analyse** and interpret business plans. (HL)

© The IBO, 2007

Decision making

Decision making is a process through which managers attempt to select a course of action from a variety of alternatives to solve a problem.

Decision-making framework
Steps involved in effective decision making

1. Identify the problem.

2. Research and gather data relating to the problem.

3. Analyse and evaluate the gathered data; evolve possible courses of action.

4. Choose a course of action and communicate it to all stakeholders who will be affected by the decision.

5. Implement the decision.

6. Evaluate the outcomes.

1. *The decision- making process is continuous as there are always improvements to be made.*

2. *Business decisions are constrained by factors within the internal and external environments.*

Decision making is aided by tools and techniques, such as PEST analysis, BCG matrix, Ratio Analysis, Decision trees and Fishbone analysis.

You must be able to **apply** a formal decision-making framework to a given situation.   © The IBO, 2007

Scientific versus intuitive decision-making processes
(HIGHER LEVEL FOCUS)

Scientific decisions are based on research, analysis and evaluation of data relevant to the specific situation. It is a rational process that leverages specific decision-making tools (e.g., PEST analysis) and takes into account all aspects of the decision to be made.

Intuitive decisions are about finding the first solution that solves the problem. Such decisions are based purely on the decision maker's gut feeling, experiences, judgement and creative abilities.

You must be able to **compare** and **contrast** scientific and intuitive decision-making.   © The IBO, 2007

Fishbone/Cause-and-effect analysis
(HIGHER LEVEL FOCUS)

Kaoru Ishikawa suggested that issues relating to **people, materials, machine** and **methods** are the root causes of problems in any organisation. Fishbone analysis helps managers to illustrate the root causes and effects of a problem.

Some other root causes can be attributed to current or changing procedures and policies, and changing circumstances within the external environment.

The fishbone

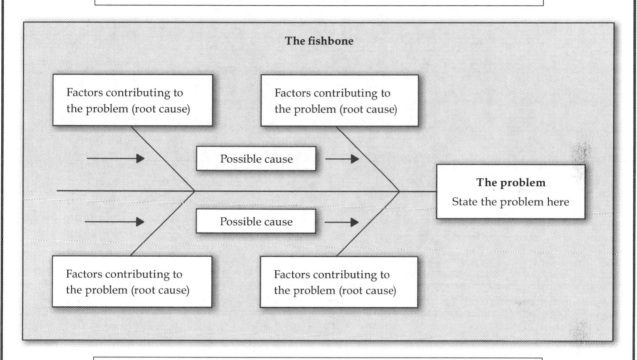

Benefit and limitation of Fishbone analysis

Once all the causes of the problem are identified and categorised, those which are crucial to the decisionmaking process are further analysed and evaluated.

Benefit

The Fishbone model is a good tool to use while trying to identify the possible causes of a problem. All opinions are considered and added to the diagram.

Limitation

Fishbone analysis is a time-consuming process; moreover, not all the identified causes may be of concern.

You must be able to **apply** decision-making processes and planning tools (for, e.g. fishbone).

Decision trees
(HIGHER LEVEL FOCUS)

A decision tree is a decision-making model that can be used to illustrate the alternative courses of actions which can be taken towards a decision.

Constructing a decision tree

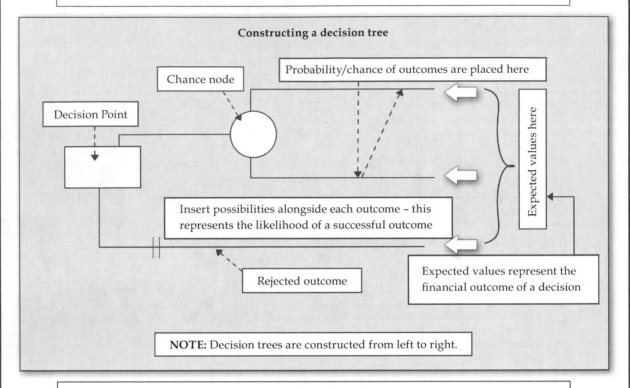

Chance node

Decision Point

Probability/chance of outcomes are placed here

Expected values here

Insert possibilities alongside each outcome – this represents the likelihood of a successful outcome

Rejected outcome

Expected values represent the financial outcome of a decision

NOTE: Decision trees are constructed from left to right.

Features of a decision tree

Decision point: The position from which the decision is to be taken.

Chance node: Represents the likelihood of an event being successful or unsuccessful.

Expected value: The financial outcome associated with a decision.

An example of how decision trees can help manager to make effective decisions

The management of Caribbean Traders Plc must decide whether or not to launch a new classic sofa bed collection for the Christmas season. The new product could be launched by giving a free gift with every purchase. However, this strategy will cost the firm $15000 and the market research team has estimated that the product has a 60% chance of success. The market research team has also estimated that the product has a 40% chance of success if it is launched without the free gift option. A successful launch will earn the company an estimated $100,000 profit. On the other hand, management expects an earning of $45,000 if the launch is unsuccessful.

Using the information presented above we can now:

1. Construct a decision tree for Caribbean Traders Plc.
2. Calculate the expected values (Financial outcomes) of each option
3. Advise management on the best course of action.

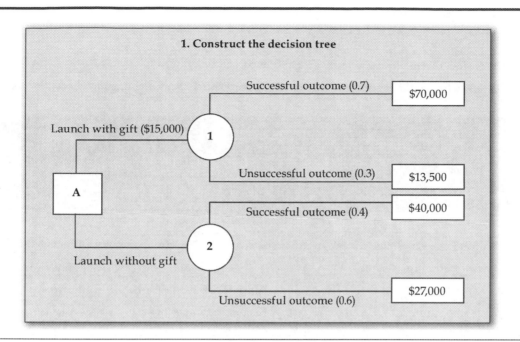

1. Construct the decision tree

Launch with gift ($15,000) — Node 1
- Successful outcome (0.7) → $70,000
- Unsuccessful outcome (0.3) → $13,500

Launch without gift — Node 2
- Successful outcome (0.4) → $40,000
- Unsuccessful outcome (0.6) → $27,000

A

---

2. Calculate the expected values

Expected Value = Probability of an event occurring × Expected Results

Calculating the expected value for the launch with the gift option

Expected value for node 1 = (0.7 × $100,000) + (0.3 × $45,000) ⟹ $70,000 + $13,500 = $83,500

NOTE: As an expense of $15,000 is associated with this option, the expense value should be subtracted from $83,500. Therefore, $83,500 - $15,000 = $68,500

Calculate expected value for the launch without the gift option

Expected value for node 2 = (0.4 × $100,000) + (0.6 × $45,000) ⟹ $40,000 + $27,000 – $67,000

---

3. Make a decision on the most viable option

On financial grounds, when we compare the outcomes of launching the product with a free gift and launching it without a free gift, the first option seems more viable and hence should be considered.

Advantages of decision trees

√ Help predict the future

√ Help depict the various options or courses of action available to decision makers, particularly when resources are limited

√ Enable decision makers to identify the financial gains or risks associated with a decision

√ Provide a framework to quantify the values of outcomes and the probabilities of achieving them

Disadvantages of decision trees

√ Do not consider the qualitative factors which may impact a chosen course of action

√ Results can be flawed if the values associated with the various outcomes are not properly determined

---

You must be able to:

1. **Construct** and interpret decision trees.

2. **Critically evaluate** the value of decision trees as a decision-making tool.

© The IBO, 2007

Internal and external constraints on decision making

Some internal constraints	Some external constraints
√ Availability of finance	**Political:** Legal policies, nature of government
√ Organisational culture	**Economic:** Change in interest rates, economic growth or decline
√ Organisational structure	**Social/Cultural:** Change in attitudes and lifestyles
√ Attitudes	**Technological:** Change in production technology
√ Corporate objectives	

SWOT analysis

SWOT is an acronym for a firm's internal **Strengths** and **Weaknesses** and external **Opportunities** and **Threats**. It is an audit of a firm's internal competitive advantage (Strengths) and negative factors (Weaknesses) and the external elements which are favourable (Opportunities) or hostile (Threats) towards its development.

Preparing a SWOT analysis

Managers preparing SWOT analysis for their companies may consider the following questions regarding each element of the audit.

Strengths	Weaknesses
√ What advantages does the company have?	√ What disadvantages does the company have in relation to its rivals?
√ What is the company doing better than its rivals?	√ What are the factors contributing to poor perception and corporate image?
√ What is the company's Unique Selling Proposition (USP)?	√ What are the factors responsible for the high attrition rate?
√ How financially stable is the company?	√ What are the factors limiting the firm's ability to differentiate its products and services?
√ What is the public perception of the company?	√ Why is cost of production higher than that of competitors?

Opportunities	**Threats**
√ How is technology changing and what benefits is the change bringing to the business?	√ What changes in the external environment does the company face?
√ What new government legislation favours the business?	√ Is the firm under threat of a takeover bid?
√ What opportunities for growth exist?	√ How are competitors taking advantage of the firm's weaknesses?
√ What opportunities are presented by new economic and market trends, fashions, and positive behaviours?	√ Is the company finding it difficult to access finance?
√ What opportunities are available for partnerships with the community?	√ Is share price falling?
√ Are rivals leaving the industry?	

You must be able to **prepare** a SWOT analysis for a given situation. © The IBO, 2007

The SWOT analysis of a firm might indicate the following

Internal

Strengths: Positive factors	**Weaknesses: Negative factors**
√ Good customer service	√ Many defective products
√ Financial stability	√ Poor quality control
√ Strong R&D	√ Rigid organisational structure
√ Committed employees	√ Limited employee benefits
√ Largest market share	√ Highly geared operation
	√ High attrition rate

External

Opportunities: Positive factors	**Threats: Negative factors**
√ Expanding industry	√ Growing number of competitors
√ Government incentives for diversification	√ Changing consumer taste
√ Very few competitors in the market	√ Impact of pressure groups
√ Positive sustainable growth in the economy	√ Economic recession
√ Dropping interest rates	√ Overtrading

You must be to **analyse** an organisation's position using a SWOT analysis. © The IBO, 2007

1.7: GROWTH AND EVOLUTION

Economies and diseconomies of scale

Economies of scale: As a firm grows in size (increased output), it is able to lower its unit cost of production, due to a number of factors which are collectively referred to as **Economies of Scale**.

Internal economies of scale

Internal economies of scale refer to factors which result in the cost savings that accrue to individual firms because they operate on a large scale. Internal economies of scale are classified as follows:

√ Technological economies of scale

√ Financial economies of scale

√ Managerial economies of scale

√ Purchasing economies of scale

√ Marketing economies of scale

√ Risk-bearing economies of scale.

Technological economies of scale

The firm is able to benefit from the use of equipment and technology to enhance output and efficiency.

Following are some examples of technological economies of scale from which large firms benefit:

√ Technical training for employees

√ Advanced communication technology

√ Mechanised and automated production systems

√ Technology upgrades

√ Effective production processes

√ Efficient quality-control systems.

Managerial/Administrative economies of scale

Large firms benefit from employing managers with specialist expertise. Following are some examples of managerial economies from which large firms benefit:

√ Specialisation and division of managerial functions

√ Delegation of authority

√ Functional departments based on managerial expertise

√ A pool of expert managers who can train employees.

Marketing economies of scale

Large firms are able to reduce cost because they can benefit from marketing economies such as:

√ Bulk purchases

√ Efficient supply-chain management

√ Low advertising and promotional costs

√ Better pricing structure for products and services.

√ Distribution outlets

√ Well-established brands

Financial economies of scale

As large firms enjoy financial stability and access to financing, they can benefit from financial economies which include:

√ Multiple sources of funding

√ Less-apparent financial risk when compared with smaller firms

√ Opportunities to float on the stock market.

√ Strong and adequate collateral

√ Authority to negotiate with financiers of investment projects

Risk-bearing economies of scale

As a large firm is in a position to diversify into other areas of business it can benefit from risk – bearing economies which include:

√ Opportunities for diversifying into other business interests

√ Mergers and acquisitions

√ Joint ventures and strategic alliances.

Purchasing economies of scale

Purchasing economies from which large firms benefit:

√ Bulk purchase of raw materials

√ Authority to negotiate with suppliers

√ Reduced costs of raw materials and components

√ Reasonable credit terms from suppliers.

External economies of scale

Average cost of production decreases due to the increasing size of the industry. Examples of external economies of scale:

√ Availability of knowledgeable, experienced and qualified labour

√ Shared infrastructure, research and development

√ Technological advances and collaboration on key projects

√ Establishment of service firms

√ Shared training facilities.

Internal and external diseconomies of scale

When a firm outgrows its optimum capacity, it begins to experience diseconomies of scale. That is, its average cost of production begins to rise. Diseconomies of scale result from the following factors:

√ Communication problems

√ Overcrowding within the industry

√ Lack of coordination and control

√ Too much bureaucracy

√ Insufficient funding to support planned expansion projects.

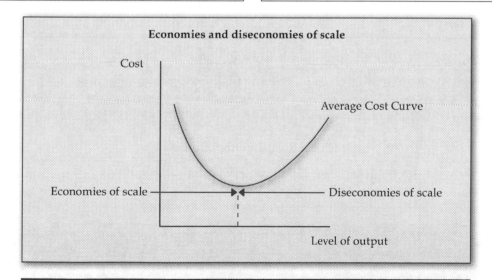

Economies and diseconomies of scale

You must be able to **apply** the concepts of economies and diseconomies of scale to business decisions.

© The IBO, 2007

Small versus large organisations

Measures of business size

The size of a business can be determined by a number of factors:

- √ Market capitalisation
- √ Number of employees
- √ Profitability
- √ Level of automation and mechanisation
- √ Number of outlets
- √ Sales revenue.

Merits of small organisations

- √ Willingness to sell products and services which are usually not provided by large businesses
- √ Lower cost of production
- √ Operate in small, specialised markets with limited demand
- √ Flexibility (Examples: easily adapt to changing market conditions, accommodate customers requests, flexible working hours)
- √ Benefit from government programmes which encourage the growth of small businesses
- √ Provision of employment

Demerits of small organisations

- √ Restricted access to funding
- √ Absence of economies of scale
- √ Limited managerial expertise
- √ Competition from larger firms

Merits of large organisations

- √ Considerable benefits from economies of scale and scope
- √ Ability to offer a diversified range of products and services, shopping conveniences, and price discounts
- √ Stimulus for economic growth

Demerits of large organisations

- √ Inflexibility and slowness in responding to changing market conditions
- √ Threat of diseconomies of scale

You must be able to:

1. **Evaluate** the relative merits of small vs. large organisations.
2. **Recommend** an appropriate scale of operation for a given situation.

© The IBO, 2007

Internal and external growth: The differences

Internal/Organic growth

The process where a business grows through one or more strategies, for example:

√ Evolving new products and services

√ Increasing market share

√ Increasing sales revenue and profits

√ Setting up a new branch

√ Employing new technology.

External/Inorganic growth

The process where a business grows by merging with or acquiring other businesses. Examples include:

√ Joint ventures

√ Strategic alliances

√ Mergers and acquisitions

√ Franchises.

Advantages of organic growth

√ Corporate culture is kept intact

√ Encourages internal innovation

√ Ownership and control is not diluted

√ Full control over activities

√ Security for employees

Disadvantages of organic growth

√ Slow method of growth

√ Very expensive

√ High risk

√ Limited growth options

You must be able to **explain** the difference between internal and external growth. © The IBO, 2007

External growth: Joint venture

Joint venture is a partnership in which two or more firms collaborate by sharing expertise, resources and control on a specific business venture. The joint venture is established as a separate legal business entity.

Advantages

√ Effective pooling of resources and expertise

√ Access to sources of local raw materials

√ Market penetration – increased market share

√ Economies of scale and scope

√ Entry into international markets

√ Less competition

Disadvantages

√ Reluctance of partners to share technology

√ Organisational and cultural differences

√ Communication hassles

√ Prolonged decision making

√ Involved parties must be fully committed for the joint venture to succeed

External growth: Strategic alliance

A strategic alliance is collaboration where two or more business entities operate a venture towards a common goal – profit. Unlike joint venture, a strategic alliance is not a separate business entity.

Advantages

√ Possibility of overcoming the limitations experienced by small-size firms

√ Opportunity for innovation, research and development, growth

√ Sharing risks associated with the project

√ More access to facilities, technology and expertise

√ Access to new markets

Disadvantages

√ Difficulty in identifying compatible business partners

√ A small company may be dominated by its larger partner

√ Profits must be shared

√ Cultural differences and communication hassles

External growth: Merger/Integration

A merger/integration is a mutually agreed combination of two or more businesses into a single entity.

Advantages

√ Synergy	√ Larger market share
√ Rapid corporate growth	√ Larger amounts of capital
√ Economies of scale and scope	√ Shared management expertise
√ Increased shareholders' value	

Disadvantages

√ Culture clash	√ Job losses
√ Organisational restructuring	√ Diseconomies of scale
√ Fewer firms: Less choices for customers	√ Lower prices for suppliers
√ Complacency, due to limited competition	

Types of mergers/integration

Type	Description	Examples
Horizontal	Merger between companies operating at the same level of production in the same industry.	A merger between two firms in the airline industry, e.g., the recent merger between Northwest Airlines and United Airlines.
Vertical	**Forward:** A firm merges with the distributor of its products.	A bakery merging with the distributor of its products.
	Backward: A firm merges with the supplier to reduce dependency.	A merger between a bakery and the supplier from which it purchases the flour to make its products.
Conglomerate	One company owning many companies in varied, unrelated industries.	Samsung and General Electric Co. are examples of conglomerates.

Advantages and disadvantages of merger/integration

Type	Advantages	Disadvantages
Horizontal	Greater market share Access to new skills and expertise Economies of scale and scope Greater investment in R&D	Seen as anti-competitive Loss of jobs for employees Higher prices for customers
Vertical	**Forward** Better control over pricing Increased control over distribution Employees benefit – job security	Possibility of higher prices for consumers Risk of overtrading Employees may lack job security
	Backward Reduced dependency on suppliers Increased control over procuring raw materials Control over the price of stocks	Threat of monophony Threat to competitors Possibility of closer government scrutiny
Conglomerate	Economies of scale Economies of scope	Competition for limited resources Likelihood of diseconomies of scale

External growth: Takeover

A takeover occurs when one company acquires the control of another company. Takeovers are regarded as the most aggressive form of external growth and can be **hostile** or **friendly** in nature.

Why do firms favour this method of growth?

√ Increase in market share – market dominance

√ Acquisition of expertise and skills

√ To acquire a competitor for less than its real value

√ Diversification in operations, products and services

√ Economies of scale and scope

√ Elimination of competition

√ Increase in share value

Why do some companies become takeover targets?

√ Have goodwill in the market (example, an excellent brand name)

√ Partly owned by a stronger company   √ Operate in niche markets

√ Have knowledgeable and qualified managers   √ Have financial problems

√ Have strong customer base and market share   √ Want to sell off non-core businesses or activities

You must be able to:

1. **Evaluate** joint ventures, strategic alliances, mergers and takeovers as methods of achieving a firm's growth objectives.

2. **Evaluate** internal and external growth strategies as methods of business expansion (HL students only)

© The IBO, 2007

Porter's generic strategies
(HIGHER LEVEL FOCUS)

Porter's generic model outlines three strategic options which are available to businesses seeking sustainable competitive advantages in the industry in which they operate.

     1. Cost leadership   **2. Differentiation**   **3. Focus**

Cost-leadership strategies

Cost-leadership strategies position a business as the low-cost producer of the industry in which it operates. Adopting these strategies, however, does not mean that the firm should not aim to be efficient and profitable. Some examples of cost-leadership strategies are:

√ Adopting new technologies before competitors do   √ Sourcing quality, low-cost suppliers

√ Enhancing the efficiency of operational process   √ Merging with or acquiring key suppliers

√ Outsourcing, subcontracting, or both   √ Downsizing the organisation structure.

Differentiation strategies

Differentiation strategies are aimed at giving a firm's products and/or services sustainable competitive advantage. Following are some areas in which a firm can differentiate:

     √ Pricing   √ Location

     √ Branding   √ Sale of the product

     √ CSR initiatives   √ Customer relations

     √ Any aspect of the physical product or service (e.g., product design).

Focus strategies/Niche strategies

Focus strategies are concentrated on well researched and defined segment of the market which is not very competitive but presents considerable opportunities.

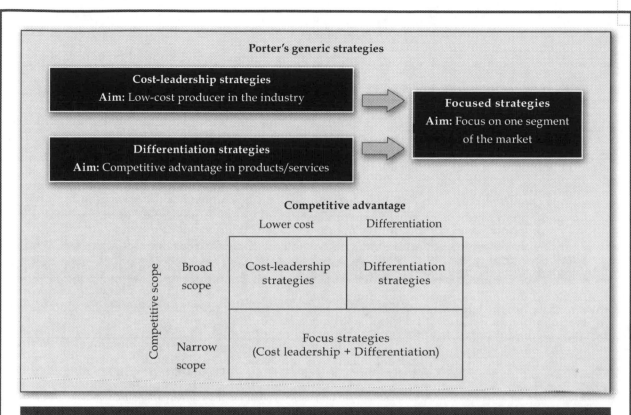

Franchises

Franchise is a licensing agreement between a **franchisor** and a **franchisee**. In return for a franchise fee and ongoing royalty payments, the franchisee is permitted to use the franchisor's brand name as a means of authenticating and supporting her business.

Advantages

√ Established brand-name recognition (Franchisee)

√ Support from franchisor (Franchisee)

√ National and international expansion (Franchisor)

√ Increase in revenue (Franchisor)

Disadvantages

√ Franchisee has little creative control

√ Franchise cost can be very expensive

√ Franchisee may fail to maintain the franchisor's standards

√ Not all franchises are successful

The Ansoff matrix

Value of Ansoff matrix as a decision-making tool

The Ansoff matrix, is a valuable tool for mapping the growth strategies available to a firm.

Value: The Ansoff Matrix is a tool which can be used by businesses to map their growth strategy. The tool focuses on four strategic options: **Market Penetration, Market Development, Product Development,** and **Diversification.**

Limitation: The use of the Ansoff matrix by itself does not guarantee the success of a chosen strategy. As a result, whenever a firm makes a strategic decision regarding its market or products, other activities, such as SWOT and PEST analyses are conducted.

You must be able to **explain** the value of the Ansoff matrix as a decision-making tool.   © The IBO, 2007

Application of the Ansoff matrix

PRODUCTS

	Present	New
Present (MARKETS)	**Market Penetration** Selling more of the existing products in the existing markets. **Examples of strategies** √ Improving product quality. √ Gaining competitors' customers. √ Cutting prices or giving special offers. √ Sales promotion. **Low-risk growth strategy**	**Product Development** New products for existing markets **Examples of strategies** √ Develop related products. √ Enhance existing products. √ Develop a totally new product. **Medium-risk growth strategy**
New (MARKETS)	**Market development** Attracting new markets for existing products. **Examples of strategies** √ Promote the product in new market segments. √ Use various market channels. √ Offer free, limited trials. √ Offer price discounts. **Medium-risk growth strategy**	**Diversification** New products are developed for new markets. **Examples of strategies** √ **Related diversification:** Same market, same industry – Horizontal, vertical integrations. √ **Unrelated diversification:** Outside of current industry or market – conglomerate integration. **High-risk growth strategy**

You must be able to **apply** the Ansoff-matrix growth strategies to a given situation.   © The IBO, 2007

1.8: CHANGE AND MANAGEMENT OF CHANGE
(HIGHER LEVEL FOCUS)

Change is a transformation process that an organisation goes through in response to variations in the internal and external environments.

The causes of change: Examples

√ Changing technology

√ People: Management, employees, customers

√ Changing social and economic trends: National and international

√ Government legislation

√ Mergers and acquisitions

√ Reorganisation of administrative processes

Factors causing resistance to change: Examples

√ Failure to discuss change initiatives with those affected by the change

√ Inadequate rewards associated with the change

√ Inadequate training

√ Uncertainty

√ Ineffective leadership

√ Workers' attitude towards change

You must be able to **explain** the causes of change and the factors causing resistance to change.

© The IBO, 2007

Modelling change

Force-field analysis is a useful decision-making tool for evaluating the forces which can propel or restrain a change initiative.

Lewin force field model

Driving forces: Forces for success

√ Profitability

√ Sales revenue

√ Efficiency

√ Incentives

√ Image and reputation

√ Positive economic trends

Change initiative

Restraining forces: Forces against success

√ Increasing costs

√ Pressure groups

√ Poor location

√ Poor attitude towards change

√ Negative economic trends

Unfreezing: Unlearning and undoing the *old ways* of doing things. It involves activities, such as educating, presenting evidence and restructuring.

Change: This phase is about moving towards the desired change. It involves implementing personal and organisational changes. For e.g., changes in attitudes, behaviour and technology.

Refreezing: The process of monitoring the expected results associated with the change initiative. It involves reinforcing change, so that it becomes fully institutionalised.

You must be able to **examine** the dynamic nature of organisations and the relative importance of driving and restraining forces.

© The IBO, 2007

Strategies for reducing the impact of change and resistance to change

Some unfreezing strategies

√ Education – communicate the need for and benefits of the change initiative

√ Consultation and facilitation

√ Restructuring

√ Presenting evidence of past successes

Some change/movement strategies

√ Incentives

√ Adequate, sustained training effort

√ Peer support

√ Adequate resources

√ Phased implementation of the change

√ Coercion

Some refreezing strategies

√ Eliminate the *old ways*

√ Give incentives

√ Celebrate successes

√ Communicate results

√ Institutionalise the change

√ Set well-defined standards

You must be able to **evaluate** different strategies for reducing the impact of change and resistance to change.

© The IBO, 2007

1.9: GLOBALISATION

Globalisation refers to the movement of the world towards political, economic, social and technological integration.

Multinational companies

Multinational companies (MNC) are businesses which have their head offices in one country and a presence in two or more other countries. Examples include Nokia, KFC, Nike and Microsoft.

Some reasons for growth of multinational companies

√ Globalisation of markets

√ Financial leverage e.g., some multinational companies are richer than some governments

√ Lucrative incentives offered by governments of host countries

√ Environmental policies of their home countries drive companies to have a presence in countries where policies are not so stringent

√ Cost of labour e.g., one of the factors which have contributed to the growth of multinational companies in China is the low-labour cost

Some problems in the development of a multinational company

A company seeking a presence outside its home country should consider the following factors with respect to the host country:

√ Political stability

√ Adequate infrastructure, such as communication systems and roads

√ Economic factors, such as currency exchange and interest rates, ability to repatriate profits

√ Culture and language

√ Qualifications, experience and expertise of the available workforce.

You must be able to **discuss** reasons for the growth of multinational companies. © The IBO, 2007

The role played by multinationals in the global business environment

Multinational companies conduct the following functions within an international context:

√ Provide jobs

√ Drive technological change and innovation

√ Bring much-needed Foreign Direct Investments (FDI). Millions of dollars are invested by companies, such as Microsoft, in new and existing projects in some of their host countries

√ Contribute to community development through their Corporate Social Responsibility initiatives

√ Drive the world economy.

You must be able to **analyse** the role played by multinationals in the global business environment.

© The IBO, 2007

The impact of multinational companies on the host country

Multinational companies have both positive and negative impacts on host countries.

Some positive impacts	Some negative impacts
√ Transfer of technology and other assets	√ Pollution
√ Provision of employment and training	√ Exploitation of labour force
√ Community development	√ Unreasonable exploitation of natural resources
√ Contribution to economic development	√ Competition for local businesses
√ Improved standards of living	√ Unemployment
√ Foreign Direct Investments (FDIs)	

You must be able to **evaluate** the impact of multinational companies on the host country.   © The IBO, 2007

Regional trading blocs

Regional trading blocs are intergovernmental agreements within geographic regions in which participating countries enjoy preferential treatment in trade and other activities.

Types of economic trading blocs

√ **Free Trade Area (FTA):** Member countries agree to free trade among themselves. For example, NAFTA is a free-trade agreement between Canada, Mexico and the USA.

√ **Customs Union:** All members agree to standardised trade policies, such as a common, external tariff. For example, Southern African Customs Union (SACU).

√ **Common Market:** Members of a common-market union agree to a common external tariff, plus the free movement of labour and resources amongst member countries. For example, the Caribbean Common Market (Caricom).

√ **Economic Union:** Member countries adopt policies, such as common external tariffs, free movement of labour and capital, and a common currency. For example, the European Union (EU).

Some impacts on business of a country that is a member of a regional economic bloc

1. Wider customer base

2. Reduction in business-transaction costs, with a single currency

3. Stability and ease of trading

4. Deal with protective trade barriers outside of the trading bloc

5. Expense of importing raw materials and components from outside of the trading bloc

6. Competition to domestic firms

You must be able to **explain** the impact on business of a country that is a member of a regional economic bloc.

© The IBO, 2007

2.1: HUMAN-RESOURCE PLANNING

Human resource planning is a key organisational function which ensures that competent people are employed and retained. Human resource planning is concerned with issues such as the following:

√ Recruitment   √ Retention

√ Training   √ Staff Appraisals

√ Employee benefits   √ Settlement of dispute

√ Dismissals/retrenchment.

The supply of human resources

The number of people available for work at any point in time is affected by changes in the structure of the population (demographic changes). Some demographic variables that are likely to affect the supply of labour are as follows:

√ Age (e.g., school leaving and retirement age)

√ Gender (e.g., the extent to which women participate in the workforce)

√ Migration: Domestic or international movement of people

√ Level of unemployment

√ Education (e.g., the availability of highly skilled graduates)

√ Population growth or decline.

Constraints and opportunities posed by demographic changes

Demographic change	Possible constraints	Possible opportunities
Age For example, retirement age increase from 55 to 60.	Increase in cost of medical benefits. The need to reduce work hours. The reluctance of older workers to embrace change.	Older employees connect with the organisation's culture. Older employees have considerable experience and expertise from which the organisation benefits. Older employees bring stability to the workforce.
Gender For example, more women seeking employment.	The gender can influence the level of absenteeism and the number of part time workers, depending on family status and culture.	With both men and women seeking employment, employers have a wider variety of skills and expertise to choose from.
Migration For example, movement of labour from one country to another (geographic mobility).	The need to develop and implement training as immigrants may not have the required skills.	The relative supply of labour is increased. Employers can pay substandard wages to immigrants (although this practice may be illegal in some countries).

You must be able to **identify** the constraints and opportunities provided by demographic changes.

Workforce planning

Workforce planning is about preparing for changes in the workforce. Such changes range from increase in the size of the business to retirement of long serving employees.

Following are some of the factors that influence the workforce planning process adopted by a business:

√ Attrition rate

√ Objectives of the business

√ Rate at which the business grows e.g., technological changes, increases in sales

√ Competition

√ State of the economy

√ Mobility of the workforce.

Stages in the workforce planning process

1. Defining the strategic goals of the business

2. Conducting a workforce need analysis, e.g., number of workers leaving, number of new workers needed, skills required

3. Developing an action plan, e.g., domestic or overseas recruitment, need for training

4. Implementing the action plan, e.g., advertise the position, select, recruit, train

5. Reviewing the action plan

NOTE: A major part of workforce planning is about comparing the available human resources with what will be required in the future.

The impact of labour mobility

Labour mobility refers to the movement of labour across geographic locations (domestic and international) and between jobs (Occupational mobility).

1. Enables employers to exploit new skills and quickly fill vacancies

2. Provides skilled workers the opportunity to practise their trade across domestic and international regions and across occupations

3. Fosters political and socio-economic integration amongst members of economic blocs, such as the European Union and Caricom

4. Improves the financial status of workers

5. Delays the rise in wage rates

Labour mobility has several disadvantages, with one such disadvantage being the unfair exploitation of labour by some businesses, e.g., paying substandard wages to immigrant workers, depriving immigrants of certain benefits.

The benefits of workforce planning

√ Organisations get a clear picture of their human resource needs.

√ Recruitment goals are aligned with organisational objectives.

√ Human resource needs can be addressed in a timely and effective manner.

You must be able to **discuss** the significance of changes in labour mobility, both domestic and international.

Strategies for developing future human resources

1. Developing a comprehensive plan to address the human resource needs of the organisation. The plan must focus on developmental aspects such as career progression, succession criteria, employee welfare and training.

2. Implementing a fair and transparent reward system: The system must address the needs of current and future human resources. It must also be flexible enough to accommodate changes in internal and external circumstances.

3. Facilitating healthy collaboration across the organisation.

4. Developing and maintaining well established processes and channels for communication and consultation.

You must be able to **compare** present human resources with future requirements and evaluate strategies for developing future human resources.

© The IBO, 2007

Methods of recruitment, appraisal, training, dismissal

Recruitment

Recruitment is the process of attracting qualified applicants to fill a vacant position. A business can recruit from amongst its existing employees (**internal recruitment**) or from sources outside of the business (**external recruitment**).

Internal recruitment

Advantages	Disadvantages
√ Cost effective and less time-consuming (when compared to external recruitment)	√ Restricts opportunities for new ideas and practices
√ Employees are already familiar with the business polices, practices and procedures	√ Limited number of candidates with required skills and experience
√ Motivates employees to strive for advancement within the business – creates a career structure	√ Possibility of resentment from unselected employees

Some methods of external recruitment

Employment agencies

Employment agencies are organisations that specialise in facilitating the recruitment and placement of employees within specific professions, e.g., Search Associates is an organization which specialises in facilitating the employment of teachers and administrators for international schools.

(Contd...)

Advantages

√ Availability of a larger pool of skilled, experienced and qualified labour

√ Shorter time associated with interviews and selection since applicants are initially vetted by the agencies

√ Recruiting expatriate workers is often best done through employment agencies

Disadvantages

√ Cost associated with recruitment through employment/placement agencies

√ Lack of in-depth knowledge and understanding of many aspects of the organisations they represent, e.g., organisational culture

---

The Internet (e-recruiting)

Some companies use the World Wide Web to attract potential candidates to fill vacant positions.

Advantages	Disadvantages
√ Cost effective and less time consuming	√ Impersonal nature of e-recruiting increases the risk of employing applicants who may not necessarily be the *best fit* for the organisation.
√ Greater geographical reach when advertising for skilled employees	√ There is the danger of being inundated with large volumes of inappropriate resumes since the vacancies are advertised globally.
√ Access to a wider pool of candidates with relevant qualifications and expertise	

Employee referrals/recommendations

This is a process where employees refer job applicants to the business for recruitment.

Advantages	Disadvantages
√ Candidates have some understanding of the organisation as they might have been briefed by the referring employee	√ Close associations present the danger of conspiracy within the workforce.
√ Cost–effective and less time-consuming	√ Accusations of discrimination in hiring policy could be levelled against management.

External recruitment

Advantages	Disadvantages
√ New ideas, focus, perspectives and practices	√ Costly and time consuming
√ Broader pool of qualified and experienced applicants	√ Difficulties in adjusting to the new organisational culture can bring down productivity
√ Flexibility in negotiating salaries and benefits	

Appraisal

Appraisal is the process of assessing and evaluating an employee's performance. Appraisals are performed for a number of reasons, including:

√ To identify training needs

√ To justify increase in wages and other benefits

√ To identify employees with the potential for promotion

√ To have employees reflect on their performance and make plans for improvements.

Some methods of employee appraisal

Management by Objectives (MBO)

Management and employee mutually agree on a set of goals to be achieved by the employee within a specified timeframe. Subsequently, the employee is evaluated based on the extent to which the goals were accomplished.

Advantages

√ Employees are motivated as they have clear goals to work towards.

√ Employee performance is evaluated based on a set of pre-defined outcomes.

Disadvantages

√ Insufficient resources can limit the employee's ability to achieve the goals.

√ Strict focus on the achievement of goals might diminish other aspects of the employee's performance.

360-degree (Multi-rater) feedback

This method of appraisal allows employees to gather feedback on their performance from their subordinates, colleagues, managers and customers. It also requires employees to conduct a self-assessment and evaluation of their own performance.

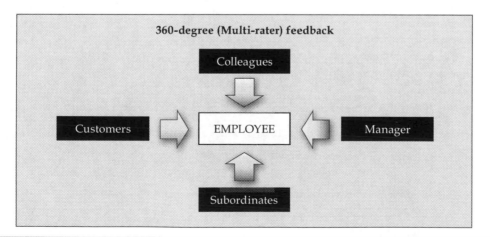

360-degree (Multi-rater) feedback

(Contd...)

Advantages

√ Employees are made aware of how they are perceived at a professional level by the people with whom they work.

√ 360-degree feedback, if conducted correctly, boosts personal and professional development of employees and management.

Disadvantages

√ The 360-degree feedback is limited to character traits and work ethics. It does not consider the achievement of concrete goals, such as meeting a specific production target.

√ Emotions, personal biases and subjective opinions may influence the feedback.

Multi-person comparison

A process that appraises an employee's performance, based on a comparison with the performances of his/her colleagues.

Advantages	Disadvantages
√ Useful for making a selection for promotion	√ Very subjective
√ Encourages competition, which results in increased productivity	√ Lacks a set of standard performance criteria

---

Other methods of appraisal

Graphic rating scale: Employee performance is appraised based on a list of standard performance outcomes which are presented on an incremental scale, e.g., work habits, quality of work, interrelationship with colleagues and preparedness for work.

Critical incidents: Performance evaluation is based on specific outcomes which are viewed by management as vital to the overall effectiveness of the organisation.

Training

Training refers to the acquisition or enhancement of knowledge, skills and competencies associated with current or future job functions.

An organisation's training programmes are aimed at developing the capacity of its human resources.

Reasons for training

√ To develop a pool of well-qualified, competent and efficient employees

√ To help employees enhance existing skills or acquire new skills

√ To boost employee confidence

√ To introduce new employees to the organisation

Benefits of training employees

√ Improves employee performance, quality and productivity

√ Enables employees to serve customers, at the highest level

√ Boosts staff motivation and morale

√ Empowers businesses to compete at the highest level

Cost of training employees

√ Businesses may have to hire temporary employees to substitute for those attending the training, resulting in increased wage bill.

√ In addition to training cost, businesses have to bear all related expenses, e.g., travel, accommodation.

√ If employees leave the firm shortly after getting trained, the firm has to bear the additional cost of training a new set of employees.

Methods of training

On-the-job training (OJT)

Training which is given to employees while they are performing their regular duties. This method of training is often used by supermarkets to train new cashiers. Examples of on-the-job training strategies include job rotation and internship.

Advantages

√ Firm saves on training costs.

√ Employees receive specific training relevant to their job functions.

√ Employees have access to the tools and methodologies necessary for their job functions.

√ Employees gain real-life experience which enhances their skills and expertise.

Disadvantages

√ If the trainers are not competent, trainees receive substandard training.

√ Trainees may get stressed out, as the training is often very intensive and the management expects them to be productive within a short period of time.

Off-the-job training

Off-the-job training takes place away from the work environment.

Advantages

√ Employees can focus on acquiring knowledge and skills, without worrying about their day–to-day job responsibilities.

√ Employees are trained by experienced professionals/ specialists.

√ Employees can engage in professional networking.

√ Participants from different organisations share their knowledge, skills and expertise in a formal or informal setting.

Disadvantages

√ Often very theoretical

√ May not be directly related to employees' job functions

√ Expensive, e.g., cost of the training programme, accommodation and travel expenses

Types of off-the-job training

√ Courses conducted by Universities and other professional organisations

√ Seminars and conferences

Dismissals

Refers to the termination of an employee's work contract due to one or more reasons:

√ Misconduct √ Negligence

√ Incompetence √ Disobedience

NOTE: Terminating a worker's employment without adequate notice and legitimate reason amounts to *unfair* or *wrongful* dismissal.

You must be able to:

1. **Describe** methods of recruitment, appraisal, training and dismissal.

2. **Discuss** the advantages and disadvantages of different methods of recruitment, appraisal and training.

© The IBO, 2007

Redundancies/retrenchment/lay-off

Redundancy occurs when employees are asked to leave their jobs due to one or more reasons:

√ The employees' skills are no longer needed by the business

√ The business does not have the money to continuing paying them

√ The business is acquired by another firm

√ The business relocates, e.g., moves overseas

√ The business closes down, e.g., due to bad economic conditions.

Methods of redundancy

Voluntary redundancy occurs when the management offers financial incentives to employees to volunteer for its redundancy programme.

Involuntary redundancy occurs when the management decides which employees must be made redundant.

Legal employment rights: The impact on a firm
(HIGHER LEVEL FOCUS)

A number of laws guarantee and protect employees' rights in their workplaces. Some rights which are guaranteed under specific laws are listed below:

√ Right to question or fight against discrimination, for e.g., racial discrimination, discrimination in wages or extending benefits

√ The right to be safe at work e.g., health and safety legislation

√ The right to question or fight against unfair dismissals and redundancies.

(Contd...)

Instituting legal employment rights: The impact on a firm

√ Reduced or no litigation costs

√ Reduced employee attrition

√ Improved staff morale and motivation

√ Enhanced corporate image

√ Fewer difficulties with recruiting employees to fill vacant positions

√ Costs associated with meeting the standards set by employee-protection legislation, e.g., some laws stipulate that employees must be paid a leave-passage allowance when they take their annual leave.

You must be able to **analyse** the impact on the firm of legal employment rights.   © The IBO, 2007

How recruitment, appraisal, training, dismissal and redundancy enable the firm to achieve workforce-planning targets
(HIGHER LEVEL FOCUS)

Recruitment enables the firm to achieve its workforce-planning targets by attracting the most qualified and experienced employees to fill vacant positions.

Appraisal enables a firm to evaluate the performance of its workforce and use the evaluation results to make decisions about training, promotions, demotions or dismissals.

Training enables a firm to develop its workforce capacity, by encouraging employees to acquire/enhance their competencies and skills. Strengthening the workforce capacity is an integral part of a firm's effort towards achieving effectiveness.

Dismissal enables a firm to get rid of dishonest or incompetent workers, resulting in a competent, honest and productive workforce.

Redundancy enables a firm to achieve workforce planning in terms of the number of workers it can afford to continue employing when it faces challenges such as fall in sales, increasing costs, downturn in the economy and the need to relocate.

Also, as a cost cutting strategy, a firm which acquires another business might make some employees of the business (it has acquired) redundant.

You must be able to **examine** how recruitment, appraisal, training, dismissal and redundancies enable the firm to achieve workforce-planning targets.

© The IBO, 2007

Changing employment: Patterns and practices

A change in employment practice is described as the transition from a traditional approach towards work to more flexible practices.

Reasons for changes in employment patterns and practices

√ Changing demographics, e.g., decrease or increase in the population, women entering the workforce

√ Changing employment-related cultural habits

√ Changes in economic structure, e.g., the economy becoming more focused on the tertiary sector

√ Businesses seeking to reduce labour costs

√ Changing technology which, for example, enables people to work from home

√ Globalisation

Changing work practices

1. **Working from home** is a situation where people use their homes as a base to conduct the activities associated with their jobs.

2. **Tele-working** enables employees to work from home, while using technology (e.g., telephones, faxes and Internet) to stay connected with their organisations.

3. **Flexi-time work** allows employees to choose when they start and finish work. The agreement is limited to certain conditions dictated by management.

4. **Part-time work** allows employees to work for *less-than-normal* hours.

Work patterns and practices: Consequences for employers and employees

Work pattern/practice	Consequence for employees	Consequence for employers
Working from home	Flexible work hours allow for taking care of other commitments, e.g., family responsibilities No one to consult immediately if faced with a work-related problem	May not have to extend all benefits Limited control over employees' work pattern
Tele-working	Less time at the office, fewer distractions from co-workers Distractions at home may affect the time set aside for work	Reduced spending on office space, electricity, repair and maintenance Limited control over employees' work schedule and conduct
Flexi-time work	Some freedom to choose their hours of work More time for pursuing professional development interests Brings some balance to work and family life	An attractive benefit to potential employees More focused on the individual rather than on a culture of working as a team

Work pattern/practice	Consequence for employees	Consequence for employers
Part-time work	Better balance in work and personal life	Enhanced productivity, motivation and retention
	Part-time employees may not qualify for statutory benefits e.g., state pension	Increase in cost, since in some countries, e.g., in the UK, parttime workers have the same rights as full-time workers

You must be able to:

1. **Describe** the reasons for changes in work patterns and practices and the consequences of these changes for employers and employees.

2. **Analyse** the reasons for changes in work patterns and practices and the consequences of these changes for employers and employees. **(HL Only)**

© The IBO, 2007

Charles Handy's Shamrock Organisation

(HIGHER LEVEL FOCUS)

The Shamrock Organisation is made up of three types of human resources:

1. Workers employed on a permanent, full-time basis
2. Workers employed on a short-term or part-time basis
3. Contractors to whom special jobs are outsourced.

You must be able to **apply** appropriate management theories, such as Handy's Shamrock Organisation.

© The IBO, 2007

2.2: ORGANISATIONAL STRUCTURE

An organisational structure is a framework which allows management to control the functions of departments and employees. It also defines the levels of hierarchy and responsibilities within the organisation.

The formal organisation

The following are the characteristics of a formal organisation:

√ Levels of hierarchy

√ A clear chain of command

√ Delegation of responsibilities

√ Wide or narrow span of control

√ A flat or tall structure

√ Formal rules, procedures, reporting relationships.

Delegation

Delegation refers to assigning an employee the responsibility of planning and executing a work-related task. Delegation is effective only when the employee is given the **authority, power** and **responsibility** to execute the task and is made **accountable** for every aspect of it.

Reasons for delegation

√ Reduces the manager's workload

√ Enhances organisational effectiveness

√ Develops workforce capacity

√ Improves employee effectiveness and accountability

Span of control

Span of control represents the number of employees who report directly to one specific manager/supervisor. A manager's span of control can be **wide** or **narrow**. The larger the number of employees supervised by a manager, the wider his/her span of control.

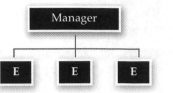

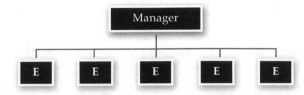

Narrow span of control   *Wide span of control*

Some factors which influence the span of control given to a manager include:

√ Physical proximity of employees   √ Managers' experience, qualifications and skills

√ Assistance available to the manager   √ Nature of the job employees are engaged in.

Levels of hierarchy/Organisational Hierarchy

In an organisation, the level of hierarchy is characterised by **superiors** and **subordinates**. Levels of hierarchy refer to the rank of employees within the organisation and are represented on an **organisational chart**.

Organisational chart

An organisational chart is the visual representation of the structure of a formal organisation. It indicates the following:

√ Hierarchical structure of the organisation

√ Positions of responsibilities within the organisation

√ Lines of communication and formal relationships.

Flat organisations

Flat organisations: Organisational structures with few levels of management.

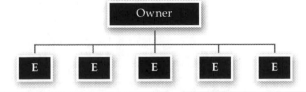

Advantages	Disadvantages
√ Faster communication and decision making	√ Suitable only for small businesses
√ Less bureaucracy	√ Manager must multi-task
√ Reduced employment costs	√ Most decisions are centralised
√ Limited or no delegation of authority	√ Wide span of control

Tall organisations

Tall organisations: Organisational structures with many levels of management.

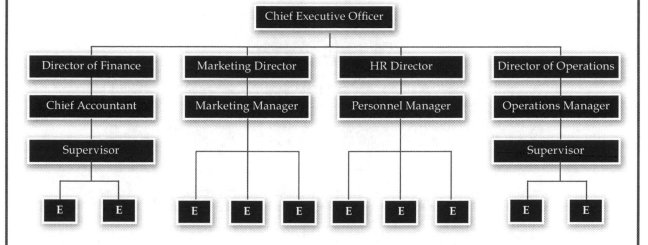

Advantages of Tall organisations	Disadvantages of Tall organisations
√ Clear management structure	√ Large administrative overheads
√ Clear lines of responsibility, authority and control	√ Slow Communication and decision making
√ Average span-of-control is narrow	√ Much bureaucracy
√ Clear path to the top	√ Limited or no delegation of authority
√ Decentralised authority	

Chain of command

The chain of command represents the line of authority which exists in the organisation.

Types of organisation (Structure)

An organisational structure is a framework through which management coordinates and facilitates formal interactions between employees and departments. Organisational structures also facilitate delegation of authority and responsibilities.

The type of organisation structure adopted by a firm depends on factors such as:

√ Corporate culture of the organisation

√ Size of the organisation, e.g., small, medium or large

√ Legal structure of the organisation, e.g., sole trader, partnership, company

√ Technology employed by the organisation

√ Objectives of the organisation

√ State of the economy.

Types of organisation (structure)

Line organisation

In a line organisation, authority flows in a hierarchy, from the highest ranked executive to the lowest level employee.

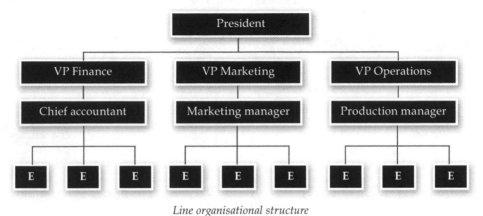

Line organisational structure

Advantages	Disadvantages
√ Clearly defines responsibilities and authority	√ Long chain of command
√ Each subordinate reports to one superior	√ Final decision rests with upper management
√ Clear lines of communication	√ Slow response time to interdepartmental problems

Functional organisations

A functional organisation is structured by departments and authority is vested with the head (manager) of each department.

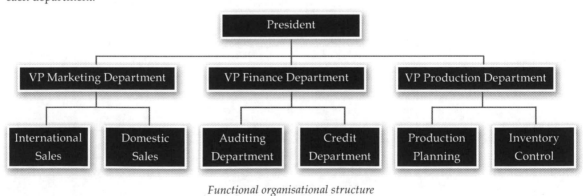

Functional organisational structure

Functional organisations

Advantages

√ Functions are coordinated within departments, resulting in effective use of resources.

√ Employees with similar interests get the opportunity to work together.

√ Functional managers are held accountable for the performance of their respective departments.

Disadvantages

√ Delay in coordination across departments.

√ Department heads/Managers are limited to their function.

√ Functional organisations are often slow in responding to changes.

Line and staff organisations

The line structure is supported by staff departments which provide specialised advice and support to line managers.

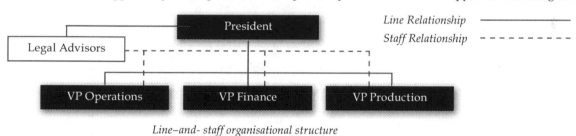

Line–and- staff organisational structure

Line-and-staff organisations

Advantages	Disadvantages
√ Line managers benefit from specialised support and advice on functions which are outside their area of expertise √ Line managers are clearly distinguished from staff advisers	√ Conflict between line and staff managers due to overlapping of authority and responsibility √ The decision making process is very slow

The nature of organisational structures

Line organisation	Line-and-staff organisation
√ Defined by clear chain of command, authority and responsibility √ Presents a top-down approach to decision making √ Structure may be tall or flat, depending on the levels of management in the organisation √ Decentralised decision making	√ Structure indicates which line functions are supported by staff specialists √ Structure is applicable to large businesses only √ The organisation chart depicts line, functional and staff authority

Functional organisation

√ Functional performance organised by departments, e.g., marketing, human resources, finance.

√ Facilitates both line and staff functions.

External factors influencing changes in organisational structure

√ **Political:** Legislation and policies can often influence business organisations. For example, increase in subsidies and reduction in corporate taxes might encourage businesses to hire more employees. Due to increased hiring, the organisation structure may change to reflect a wider span of control for existing managers.

√ **Economic:** The state of the economy can significantly influence the structure of a business. For example, while a business is likely to downsize its workforce during recession, it may hire aggressively during a period of economic growth.

√ **Social/Cultural:** The structure of a business may be influenced by the diversity of its customers. For example, a multinational company may have separate specialised divisions to serve the needs of international clients. In addition, the globalisation of labour also influences the structure of business organisations.

√ **Technological:** The adoption of technology does have a significant impact on the organisational structure of businesses. For example, the use of technology can eliminate the need for some key functions performed by employees, resulting in a flat organisational structure.

Changes in organisational structure and their effects

Internal factors influencing changes in organisational structure

√ Management objectives
√ Nature and size of the organisation
√ Diversity of the workforce
√ Organisational culture
√ The need to adopt new process/technology

Some effects of changes in an organisational structure

When the management changes the organisational structure of a business, it anticipates benefits such as the following:

√ Reduced overheads, e.g., wages and salaries

√ Improvements in the function of individuals and business units

√ Enhanced coordination and communication across the organisation

√ Centralised or decentralised authority

√ Implementation and benefit of technology.

You must be able to:

1. **Construct** different types of organisation charts and describe the nature of their structure, for example, flat, tall.

2. **Analyse** changes in organisational structures and their effects.

© The IBO, 2007

Delegation and accountability
(HIGHER LEVEL FOCUS)

Delegation: The assignment of responsibility to subordinates to undertake the planning and execution of work-related tasks.

Accountability: The requirement to act in accordance with expected behaviour or to meet expected outcomes and to give satisfactory reasons for any deviation from those expectations. For example, a subordinate to whom a task is delegated should be made to provide satisfactory reasons for any deviations from the manager's expectations.

The relationship between delegation and accountability

The manager who delegates a task must make sure of the following:

√   The task is clearly defined

√   The individual or group to which the task is delegated has the capacity to successfully accomplish the task

√   The individual or group to which the task is delegated clearly understands why they were chosen for the task

√   Expected outcomes and deadlines are clearly communicated

√   Required resources and assistance are made available.

Once these criteria are met, the manager is in a position to hold employees accountable for the success or failure of the tasks assigned to them.

Bureaucracy
(HIGHER LEVL FOCUS)

A bureaucracy is an administrative structure which is operated on formal rules and procedures and hicrarchy of authority and responsibilities. According to Max Weber (1864–1920), bureaucratic organisation are characterised by:

√   Hierarchy of authority and responsibility

√   Division of labour and specialisation

√   Formal selection of applicants for employment

√   Life-long career prospects in the organisation

√   Implementation of formal rules and procedures.

Advantages of bureaucratic structure	Disadvantages of bureaucratic structure
√ Formal rules and procedures	√ Slow communication and decision making
√ Division of labour, with clearly defined expected outcomes	√ Long chain of command and many levels of authority
√ Clear career paths	√ Duplication of authority

Some effects of organisational structure on employee motivation, communication and performance
(HIGHER LEVEL FOCUS)

Line organisational structure

Motivation

√ Clearly outlined paths to positions of authority and responsibility

√ Centralised authority can dampen employee morale.

Communication

√ Provides a framework for *top-down* as well as *bottom-up* communication

√ Helps employees understand their position and responsibility within the organisation

Performance

√ Encourages horizontal and vertical coordination of activities

√ Centralised decision making limits flexibility and creativity

Line and staff organisational structure

Motivation

√ Specialist support motivates line employees and boosts their confidence.

√ Conflicts between line and staff employees, e.g., manager and staff specialist might result in low morale and motivation.

Communication

√ Facilitates professional consultation and interaction between line/functional employees and staff specialists.

Performance

√ Availability of specialist support encourages employees to take up challenges and risks.

√ Productivity and efficiency improves.

√ Conflicts between line and staff employees might limit performance.

Functional organisational structure

Motivation

√ Employees are assigned to departments where their expertise is most needed.

√ Employees can be restricted to a particular function – de-motivating for some employees.

Communication

√ Decentralised and flexible

Performance

√ Decentralisation of authority empowers subordinates to be decision makers.

√ Competition among functional departments can hamper synergy.

You must be able to **explain** how organisational structures affect employee motivation, communication and performance.

© The IBO, 2007

Centralisation
(HIGHER LEVEL FOCUS)

Centralisation: A process of concentrating power, authority and responsibility for decision making at the top management levels.

Advantages

√ Eases coordination of activities

√ Limits duplication of activities across the organisation

Disadvantages

√ Limits the creativity and decision-making capabilities of subordinates

√ Lack of flexibility impedes the decision-making process.

Decentralisation
(HIGHER LEVEL FOCUS)

Decentralisation: A process whereby directors/managers delegate power, authority and responsibility for decision-making to subordinates.

Advantages

√ Helps the management identify and groom employees with managerial potential

√ Boosts employee motivation and performance

√ Encourages decision making at the lower levels

Disadvantages

√ Risk of incurring extra costs, e.g., cost associated with poor decisions

√ Risk of duplication of activities

Factors influencing the degree of centralisation and decentralisation
(HIGHER LEVEL FOCUS)

The following are some factors which influence the degree of centralisation and decentralisation:

√ Size of the organisation (e.g., the larger the organisation, the greater is the need to decentralise decision making)

√ Geographic dispersion of offices, outlets, branches, business activities

√ Changes in the external environment need to be responded to in a timely manner, e.g., increasing competitive pressure, globalisation, and technological changes.

You must be able to **discuss** factors influencing the degree of centralisation and decentralisation.

Matrix structure/project teams
(HIGHER LEVEL FOCUS)

The **matrix organisation** is characterised by project teams. Each team is headed by a project manager and includes employees from different departments. Team members are accountable to the Project Manager and the heads of their respective functional departments.

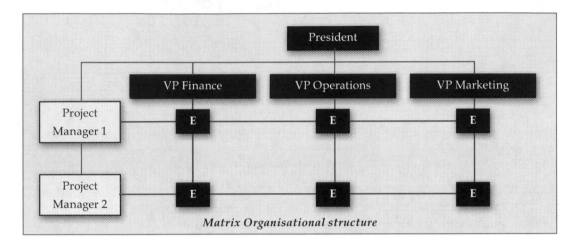

Matrix Organisational structure

Advantages

√ Allows flexibility in the use of expertise

√ Facilitates coordination and enables sharing of resources, information and expertise across the organisation (optimal use of resources)

√ Shared responsibility and authority between functional and project groups

√ Opportunities for technical training

√ Strong project focus

Disadvantages

√ Possibility of conflict between functional and project groups over authority and responsibility

√ Suitable only for project-based organisations

√ Employees are answerable to more than one boss

√ High administrative costs

Matrix organisational structure: Effects on employee motivation, communication and performance

Motivation

√ Specialist support enables teams to complete projects successfully

√ Opportunity for technical training

√ Opportunity to work on multiple projects

Communication

√ Facilitates information sharing amongst team members

√ Facilitates active development and maintenance of networks across the organisation

Performance

√ Each team member must be able to contribute to the successful completion of the project

√ Allows for integration of expertise from across the organisation

Flexible organisational structures
(HIGHER LEVEL FOCUS)

Organisations with flexible structures are well poised to respond quickly to changes within the external environment. Following are some benefits of flexible organisational structures:

√ Implement flexible work structures and practices

√ Respond quickly to changing trends, e.g., a new government policy, customers' needs

√ Develop effective systems for solving problems

√ Increase organisational competitiveness in the industry

√ Work collaboratively with other organisations to resolve issues affecting the industry

√ Empower employees

√ Decentralise the responsibility and authority for decision making.

To develop a flexible organisational structure, a business must carefully consider the extent of changes required in the following areas:

√ Management structure	√ Decision making
√ Functional relationships	√ Communication
√ Corporate culture	√ Technology
√ Size of workforce	√ Human-resource development.

Some examples of flexible organisational structures

√ The Amorphous organisational structure: Allows for work groups to be created and dissolved, based on the task that has to be completed.

√ The Matrix organisational structure.

Henry Mintzberg organisational theory (A summary)
(HIGHER LEVEL FOCUS)

1. An organisation is made up of six parts

Ideology

Techno-structure
Technical support systems, technical teams, technical analysts

Strategic Apex: Top Management

Middle Line: Middle Management

Operating Core: Operation and production processes within the organisation

Support Staff
Auxiliary staff which indirectly supports operations

NOTE: *Ideology is a representation of organisational culture.*

2. There are six basic methods for coordinating activities, processes and people across the organisation

a) Direct supervision: A top-down approach to management

b) Standardisation of work processes

c) Standardisation of output: Consistency in outcomes

d) Standardisation of skills: All workers must have the same set of skills

e) Standardisation of norms: Common set of values, norms, beliefs

f) Mutual adjustment amongst members of the organisation

3. There are six major organisational configurations

a) **Simple structure**

√ Small organisation/business

√ Top-down approach to management - coordination of activities at the tops

√ Centralised decision making

b) **Machine bureaucracy**

√ Repetition and standardisation of work processes

√ Formal rules and procedures, clear lines of authority

√ Highly specialised, automated and mechanised operation

c) **Professional organisations**

√ Standardisation of skills

√ Professionals work independently of each other

√ Decentralisation of decision making: Each professional has the decision-making authority

d) **Divisional organisation**

√ Standardisation of output

√ Diversification of functions, products, services, markets

√ Several separate divisions

e) **Ad-hocracy**

√ Decentralisation of authority and decision making

√ Accomplishment of tasks, based on mutual adjustments

√ Flexibility in responding to changing situations

√ No formal rules and procedures.

f) **Missionary organisation**

√ Principles   √ Values

√ Beliefs   √ People centred

Tom Peters organisational theory (A summary)
(HIGHER LEVEL FOCUS)

Tom Peters highlighted eight (8) themes around which flexible organisations can be developed:

1. **A basis for action:** Make the work process more flexible, through informal dialogue, information sharing and flexible rules and procedures.

2. **Close to the customer:** Focus on satisfying customers' requirements.

3. **Autonomy and entrepreneurship:** Promote excellence in employees by encouraging innovative thinking and practices; invest in the development of promising employees; take risks, without being afraid of failure.

4. **Productivity through people:** Employees are treated fairly and accorded the respect of management. Employees are to be perceived as the primary source of quality in the organisation.

5. **Hands–on, value driven:** Management leads by example; the organisation is driven by core values and principles.

6. **Stick to the knitting:** Operate within areas of core competencies.

7. **Simple form, lean staff:** Suggests flat organisational structures. Less management leads to greater flexibility.

8. **Simultaneous loose-tight properties:** Maintain core values, yet encourage autonomy, entrepreneurship, and innovation amongst employees.

You must be able to:

1. **Discuss** the development of more flexible organisational structures.

2. **Apply** the theories of writers such as Mintzberg and Peters.

© The IBO, 2007

The informal organisation
(HIGHER LEVEL FOCUS)

These are informal networks, communication structures and relationships that supplement the official organisational structure.

Characteristics of informal organisations

√ Informal relationships of people, based on their personalities and interests

√ Spontaneous relationships

√ Membership is voluntary

√ The group is driven by informal power which is vested in a few key individuals

The role and importance of informal organisations

√ Informal organisations contribute to the effectiveness of the formal organisational system. For example, they facilitate communication and improvements in productivity through direct cooperation with management.

√ Informal organizations provide an avenue for building more effective work relationships, through informal dialogue and collaboration.

(Contd...)

√ Informal organizations provide necessary psychological support to relieve members from the stress and anxiety of their job situations.

√ The cohesiveness of the group can also lead to long-term commitments to the organisation.

There are also a number of disadvantages associated with informal organisations:

√ Some informal groups are often resistant to change

√ Some work groups within the informal structure make it difficult for existing or new members to work with them.

You must be able to **evaluate** the role and importance of the informal organisation. © The IBO, 2007

The organisation of human resources

The way a firm organises its human resources is determined by factors such as:

√ Size and legal structure

√ Management objectives

√ Nature of its products and services

√ Qualifications, skills and expertise of employees.

Why do firms have to organise their human resources in particular ways?

Organisation by function

Employees with similar expertise work in the same functional department. For example, all accountants and accounts clerks work together in the accounting department. Some of the objectives of organising employees by function are listed below:

√ Concentration and coordination of skills within one functional area

√ More efficient use of resources, while holding functional managers accountable for the performance of their department

√ Employees can benefit from knowledge sharing and each others' experience and qualifications.

Following are some of the limitations of organising employees by function:

√ Delays in coordination and collaboration on cross-functional tasks and communication

√ Employees are restricted to working within their functions and areas of expertise

√ Competition amongst departments for limited resources often leads to individuals acting on their own accord rather than pursuing organisational interests.

Organisation by geography

Organisations with global reach (multinational firms) and large domestic firms organise their employees by country and regions. Some of the objectives of organising employees by geography are:

√ Meet the diverse needs of customers, in an effective and efficient manner

√ Respond to changes within the external environment in a timely and adequate manner

√ Take advantage of economies of scale and scope.

(Contd...)

Following are some of the limitations associated with organising employees by geography:

- √ Coordination and control
- √ Communication
- √ Cost.

Outsourcing, offshoring and migration of human resources
(HIGHER LEVEL FOCUS)

Outsourcing of human resources

Outsourcing refers to contracting out certain human resource functions to an external firm that specialises in performing these functions. For example, a business may outsource some functions of its finance department to a local accounting firm.

Offshoring of human resources

Offshoring refers to contracting out specific human resource functions to overseas businesses. For example, the Philippines has emerged as a leading destination for companies seeking to offshore call-centre work.

The benefits of outsourcing/offshoring human resource functions

- √ Advantage of external expertise, while reducing expenditure
- √ More time and resources available for core activities and strategic issues
- √ Greater access to technology
- √ Economies of scale and scope
- √ Improvement in quality of products and services

The limitations of outsourcing human resource functions

- √ Businesses may lose control over key functions
- √ Risk of sharing confidential information with the firm to which the job function is outsourced
- √ The growth and work-related experience of employees are restricted to a limited set of functions and processes.

The migration of human resources

Migration of human resources refers to the movement of labour either from one geographic location to another (*geographic mobility*) or across occupations (*occupational mobility*).

Migration of human resources: Positive impact on firms

√ Access to a larger, diversified, multi-skilled workforce

√ Lower cost per unit of labour

√ Diversity in the workforce, resulting in enhanced creativity, productivity and performance

√ Individuals acquire new skills

Migration of human resources: Negative impact on firms

√ Loss of valuable employees

√ Substantial costs associated with hiring and training new recruits

√ Danger of being criticised for paying substandard wages to immigrants

Summary

Following are some of the reasons behind businesses outsourcing/offshoring their human resource functions:

√ To compensate for lack of expertise in some aspects of the business process

√ To take advantages of availability of cheaper labour and technology outside of the firm

√ To concentrate limited resources and time on core activities

√ To cut back on the cost associated with some activities

√ To reduce operational costs.

The following are some of the limitations of outsourcing/offshoring human-resource functions:

√ Limited control over function

√ Possibility of a decline in employee motivation, as key functions are outsourced

√ Danger of sharing confidential information with third parties.

You must be able to:

1. **Analyse** the reasons behind, and the effects of, moving some human resource functions to external organisations located nationally or globally.

2. **Evaluate** whether firms will benefit from outsourcing, offshoring and the migration of human resource function.

© The IBO, 2007

2.3: COMMUNICATIONS

Communication is the process of sending and receiving messages. For communication to be effective, it must be clearly understood and result in some form of action.

2.3.1: The benefits of effective communication

Within a business, effective communication results in the following benefits:

√ Increased productivity

√ Enhanced corporate image

√ Better work relationships amongst employees

√ Quicker decision making

√ Healthy relationship between the business and its internal and external stakeholders.

Classification of communication

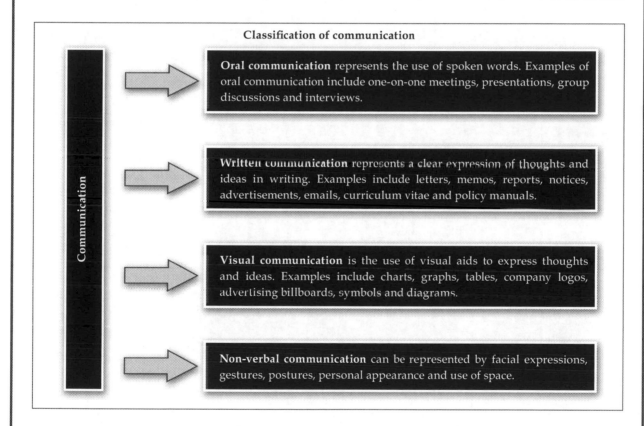

Oral communication represents the use of spoken words. Examples of oral communication include one-on-one meetings, presentations, group discussions and interviews.

Written communication represents a clear expression of thoughts and ideas in writing. Examples include letters, memos, reports, notices, advertisements, emails, curriculum vitae and policy manuals.

Visual communication is the use of visual aids to express thoughts and ideas. Examples include charts, graphs, tables, company logos, advertising billboards, symbols and diagrams.

Non-verbal communication can be represented by facial expressions, gestures, postures, personal appearance and use of space.

Classification of communication

Methods of communication	Definition	Advantages	Disadvantages
Oral	Represents the use of spoken words. Examples: one-on-one meetings, presentations, group discussions and interviews.	Message exchanged without delay. Facilitates immediate feedback. Encourages employees to hone their speaking and listening skills.	Difficult to store unless recorded. Can be distorted by noise. Time consuming.
Written	Represents clear expressions of thoughts and ideas in writing. Examples: letters, memos, reports, notices, advertisements, emails, curriculum vitae and policy manuals.	A permanent record of information. Message can be carefully written and reviewed before it is sent. Allows for well thought-out feedback. Facilitates wider transmission of information across the organisation.	Delays exchange of ideas and feedback. Delay in getting clarification on information. Inappropriate for conveying urgent messages. Reduces the possibility of face-to-face interactions.
Visual	The use of visual aids to express thoughts and ideas. Examples: charts, graphs, tables, company logos, advertising billboards, symbols and diagrams.	Transcends language and cultural barriers, enhancing the reach of the message. Message can be directed specifically to the selected audience.	Restricted to conveying the message in the present moment. Overuse can distract recipients from the intended meaning of the message.
Non-verbal	Represented by facial expressions, gestures, postures, personal appearance and use of space.	Expresses feelings, thoughts, emotions and attitude towards people or situations. Helps express empathy and maximises credibility and authority.	No records from which communication can be retrieved for future reference. Possibility of misinterpretation of expressions.

Formal communication

Formal communication is the process of following prescribed procedures to send and receive messages. Some methods of formal communication include:

√ Department and board meetings

√ Interviews

√ Financial reports

√ Official letters

√ Business-related telephone, e-mail and text messages.

Informal communication

Messages are transmitted and received through informal networks and alliances within the formal organisation structure. Examples of informal communication include:

√ Unofficial mails

√ Casual conversations amongst employees

√ Informal collaboration on a specific project or task.

Factors influencing the method of communication employed in an organisation

√ The urgency with which information must be communicated

√ The need to retrieve or refer to the information in the future

√ The nature of the information to be communicated

√ The number of recipients

√ The relationship between the sender and the recipient

You must be able to **compare** the ways in which communication takes place in organisations.

© The IBO, 2007

Organisational communication channels

Communication within an organisation can also be classified based on how it is executed.

Horizontal Communication: Exchange of information between departments.

Vertical Communication: Exchange of information between different levels of authority in the organisation, e.g., the manager giving work instructions to a subordinate.

Barriers to effective communication

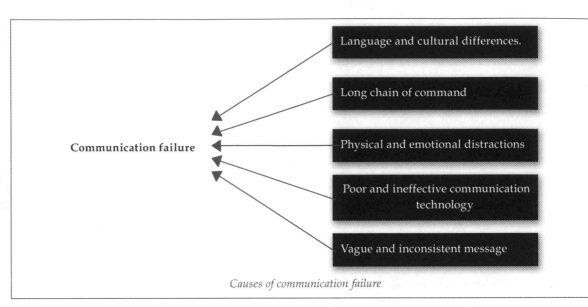

Causes of communication failure

Communication failure: Some solutions

Here are some strategies which can be adopted by businesses to prevent communication failure:

√ Adopting appropriate and effective communication technology

√ Reducing the number of levels in the organisation structure

√ Encouraging and facilitating prompt feedback

√ Adopting an open-door policy

√ Encouraging clear, accurate and consistent communication

√ Adopting a narrow span of control.

You must be able to **analyse** the causes of communication failure and evaluate the solution to such failures.

© The IBO, 2007

Forms of written communication

√ Research proposals

√ Financial reports

√ Memoranda (memos)

√ Agendas

√ Business letters

√ Business plans

√ Executive summaries

√ Resumes

Examples of different formats of business communication

The business memorandum

The business memorandum (memo) is used primarily for internal (within an organisation) communication. A sample memorandum format is given below:

Caribbean Traders Ltd

MEMORANDUM

To: Recipients' names and job titles

From: Sender's name and job title

Date: The date on which the memo is written (day, month, year)

Re: Title of the memo – a one-line description of the content

Body of the memo

√ Explains the reason for the correspondence

√ Outline specific details about the problem/requirement

√ States the action to be taken by the recipients

The business letter

The business letter is used to communicate with people or businesses outside the organisation. It is considered to be more formal than the business memorandum.

Consider the following aspects while preparing a business letter:

Business address: Should be written or printed on the organisation's letterhead

Date: Include the date on which it is written (day, month, year)

Inside address: Recipient's name and address

Salutation: Begin the letter with a formal greeting, e.g., Dear Dr. Smith or Dear Mrs. Smith

Contents: Must be clear, concise and convey the correct information

Formal closing: To end the letter, use *Yours sincerely, Best regards, Yours faithfully*

Signature: Include your full name and job title

CC: This is included if someone else is receiving a copy of the letter.

The research proposal

Consider the following points while preparing a research proposal:

1. Title of the proposal: A statement that clearly spells out the issue to be investigated

2. Issues to be investigated: Background of the problem, rationale for the study

3. An appropriate system of methods to conduct a thorough study of the topic being proposed

4. An action plan outlining activities and corresponding timelines

5. Problems which are likely to be encountered and how they will be overcome.

The research report

Consider the following sections while preparing a research report.

Title: A concise description of the primary objective of the research.

Table of contents: List of major sections in the report

Introduction: An insight into the nature and importance of the report

Executive summary: Executive summary: A brief synopsis of issues presented in the all sections of the report. It summarises the following topics:

√ *Statement of the problem*

√ *Background information*

√ *Need and significance of the issues presented in the report*

√ *The procedure adopted for gathering and analysing data*

√ *Findings*

√ *Evaluation and conclusion*

√ *Recommendations.*

Body of the report: Include as many sections as needed to present the various issues arising from the research. Some sections that may be included are:

√ *The system of method used to conduct the study*

√ *Quantitative and qualitative findings*

√ *Analyses and evaluation of findings.*

Conclusion: Issues arising from the research. Unresolved issues can also be highlighted in this section of the report.

Recommendations: Actions to be taken to address the findings presented in the report

Bibliography and references: Official sources from which information is taken

Appendices: Supporting/additional information and documents.

Agenda

The meeting agenda gives expected participants a list of items to be discussed at the proposed meeting. An agenda must include the following details:

1. **Start time:** The time when the meeting is scheduled to start

2. **Venue:** Where the meeting will be held

3. **Scope:** A list of topics to be discussed

4. **End time:** The time when the meeting is scheduled to end.

You must be able to **prepare** different forms of communication, for example, reports and research proposals.

Information and Communication Technology (ICT)

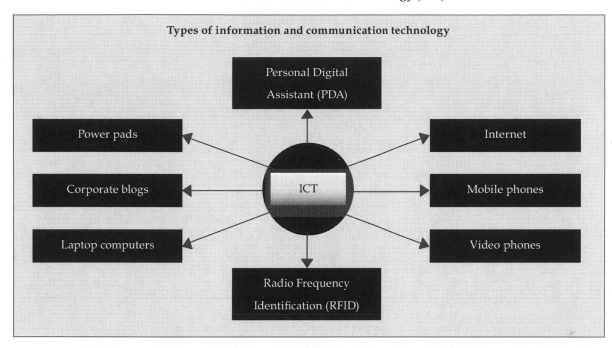

Types of information and communication technology

Personal Digital Assistant (PDA)

Power pads

Corporate blogs

Laptop computers

ICT

Internet

Mobile phones

Video phones

Radio Frequency Identification (RFID)

The impact of ICT on the effectiveness of communication between organisations and their stakeholders

Advantages

√ Facilitates effective communication

√ Enables businesses to collaborate easily and effectively on business ventures at national and international levels

√ Offers opportunities for outreach and service delivery

√ Facilitates interaction with customers and suppliers on a regular basis

√ Facilitates sharing of performance-related information with stakeholders, such as shareholders, government agencies and financial institutions

√ Speed up the communication process between organizations and their stakeholders

Disadvantages

√ Increase in training and security costs

√ Unemployment, due to downsizing or outsourcing some functions

√ Risks associated with technology, e.g., hackers accessing classified information about the organisation

Communication networks

(HIGHER LEVEL FOCUS)

Types of communication networks and their influence on the effectiveness of communication

A communication network represents the pattern of information flow. In any organisation communication networks represents the flow of information between individuals, groups or departments.

Centralised communication network

In a centralised network, communication flows through one key individual in the organisation.

The chain network: A centralised communication network

This type of communication network is typical of bureaucratic/hierarchical organisations which are characterised by formal communication where information flows from the top, down to subordinates.

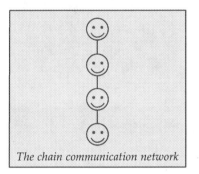

The chain communication network

The chain network: Positive impact on the effectiveness of communication

√ Enables the executive at the top of the chain to exercise total control on how and when the information is disseminated

√ Minimises conflict with regard to how and when the information is to be communicated

The chain network: Negative impact on the effectiveness of communication

√ Distortion of information (especially if the chain is very long) as it is communicated down or up the chain

√ Leader, not the subordinates, evaluates communication patterns and results

√ Leader dominates results associated with communication

The wheel network: A centralised communication network

Communication is channelled through supervisor (leader) to the rest of the group. Group members, however, are allowed to contribute their ideas on issues being addressed (for example, a sales director communicating with regional sales representatives).

(Contd...)

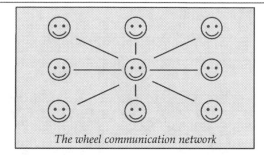
The wheel communication network

The wheel network: Positive impact on the effectiveness of communication

√ Control is vested with the leader who is positioned at the centre of the wheel.

√ Each individual in the network can have their questions addressed by the leader.

√ Each individual gets the opportunity to share his/her ideas.

√ Quick decision making is facilitated.

The wheel network: Negative impact on the effectiveness of communication

√ Leader's perceived expectations of the outcomes may not be realised.

√ Due to restricted communication flow to the network, individuals outside the network have limited opportunities to provide input.

√ Leader's ability to communicate effectively may be limited by information overload.

The 'Y' network: A centralised communication network

Information emanates from and is controlled by the leader positioned at the fork of the 'Y'. The information is then passed on to individuals or organisations within the network.

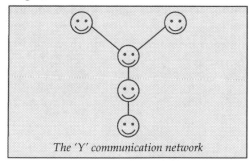
The 'Y' communication network

The 'Y' network: Positive impact on the effectiveness of communication

√ The leader can communicate the same information to a number of stakeholders simultaneously, e.g., the board of directors report on the annual performance of a company will be received by shareholders and employees at the same time.

√ Similar to the chain network, the centralised nature of the network enables the leader to control messages.

√ Communication flow and outcomes are restricted to participants in the network.

The 'Y' network: Negative impact on the effectiveness of communication

√ Lack of flexibility with regard to what message is communicated and how it is communicated.

√ Creativity and performance may be inhibited.

Decentralised communication networks

A decentralised communication network facilitates open communication amongst members.

The Circle network: A decentralised communication network

In the circle network communication is directed to one individual or department who, in turn, reciprocates.

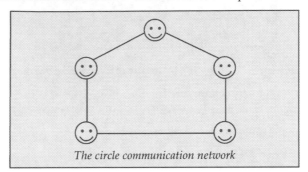

The circle communication network

The circle network: Positive impact on the effectiveness of communication

√ Enables free flow of ideas, resulting in multiple perspectives/options to address a given situation
√ Fosters interpersonal or interdepartmental relationships

The circle network: Negative impact on the effectiveness of communication

√ Discussions take a longer time, delaying decision making
√ Conflict resolution takes a longer time, inhibiting good judgement

The all-channel network: A decentralised communication network

This communication network facilitates communication among all members of the group.

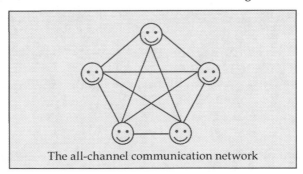

The all-channel communication network

The all-channel network: Positive impact on the effectiveness of communication

√ Opportunities for everyone to participate in the communication process to the extent of their knowledge and interest
√ Opportunities for creative thinking and solutions to problems

The all-channel network: Negative impact on the effectiveness of communication

√ Slow decision making, due to long consultation and deliberation
√ Domination of outcomes by members with strong personalities

A summary of the influence of networks on communication

	Chain	Wheel	Y network	Circle	All channel
Speed of communication	No	No	No	Yes	Yes
Information overload	Yes	Yes	Yes	No	No
Different viewpoints	No	Limited	Limited	Yes	Yes
Conflict resolution	Fast	Fast	Fast	Slow	Slow
Quality of decisions	Good	Good	Good	Better	Better
Employee motivation	Low	Low	Low	High	High

You must be able to explain how types of communication networks influence the effectiveness of communication.

© The ISO, 2007

2.4: LEADERSHIP AND MANAGEMENT

The nature of leadership

Leadership is about having the ability and power to influence others to get things done. A manager who is viewed as a good leader exhibits a combination of the following characteristics on a consistent basis:

√ A clear vision of purpose

√ The ability to foster and encourage change

√ Self-discipline and decisiveness

√ High levels of honesty and integrity

√ Knowledgeable

√ Risk-taking

√ People-centred

√ Innovative.

Leadership Styles

Autocratic leadership exercises strict control over subordinates.

Democratic leadership exhibits firm control but gives subordinates the opportunity to contribute to the decision-making process.

Laissez-faire leadership allows very high levels of flexibility by giving subordinates the opportunity to get the job done without much intervention and control. This is the most undesirable leadership style.

Situation leadership enables a leader to adopt different styles of leadership to deal with different situations.

Leadership styles: Their effectiveness and implications for organisations

Autocratic leadership

Effectiveness

√ Ideal for dealing with scenarios that warrant close supervision, e.g., training new employees

√ Ideal for crisis management and emergencies

Advantages

√ Enhances productivity if implemented in the appropriate situation

√ Helps subordinates understand what is expected of them

(Contd...)

√ Speeds up the decision-making process

√ Enables closer supervision of employees who tend to lag behind on assigned tasks

Disadvantages

√ Low employee motivation/morale

√ Reduction in productivity

√ Greater absenteeism

√ Subordinates not prepared for leadership roles

√ Limited innovation and creativity

√ High attrition rate

Democratic leadership

Effectiveness

The following are some of the situations in which this type of leadership is effective:

√ Fostering collaboration and team work

√ Gathering input from team members on the best way to approach a situation or get a job done

√ Managing subordinates who are qualified and experienced enough to work independently

√ Grooming employees for leadership roles.

Advantages

√ Boosts motivation/morale

√ Ensures job satisfaction

√ Improves quality

√ Induces commitment

√ Fosters openness, creativity and innovation

√ Leaves final decision with the leader

√ Improves management-employee relationship

Disadvantages

√ Limits the speed of the decision-making process

√ Diminishes leader's authority if he/she relies only on consultations while making a decision

√ Takes up valuable time which can rather be used to start an activity. Furthermore, not every subordinate may want to participate in the consultation process or decision making.

Laissez-faire

Effectiveness

The following are some of the situations in which this type of leadership is effective:

√ Managing employees who are experts in their respective fields and can get the job done without much interference from the manager

√ Fostering an open-door policy

√ Exercising control by outlining clear directives for the tasks to be accomplished

√ Ineffective if managers do not exercise adequate control over subordinates and their activities.

(Contd...)

Advantages

√ Subordinates who are self-starters, disciplined, knowledgeable and experienced feel empowered and motivated as they have the freedom to work without much interference from the leader.

√ Good leadership frees up the time involved in routine supervisory tasks, so the leader can focus on other aspects, e.g., planning of the department or organisation.

√ Poor leadership provides an opportunity for the subordinates to succeed the leader – formally or informally - as they look for leadership and direction.

Disadvantages

√ Low employee motivation and morale

√ Lack of authority and control results in disrespect for the leader

√ Loss of customer focus, as products and services may be of poor quality

√ Low productivity

√ Poor decision making

Situation leadership

Effectiveness

Situation leadership is effective when subordinates are at different levels of expertise, qualifications and experience.

Advantages

√ Skilled managers handle subordinates with varying supervisory needs

√ Improved productivity and quality

√ Flexible management style

√ Better communication may result

√ Higher levels of employee motivation may result

Disadvantages

√ Can be very demanding/taxing for the leader/manager

√ Can have negative implications if the leader/manager is unable to handle a diverse group of subordinates

---

You must be able to **evaluate** the effectiveness of various styles of leadership and their implications for organisations.

© The IBO, 2007

Trait and situation theories

(HIGHER LEVEL FOCUS)

A summary of trait theory

Trait theory is based on the principle that individuals are born with certain characteristics which enable them to become proficient leaders. The underlying assumption is that successful leadership in any situation is dependent on the natural skills and ability with which the leader is born.

(Contd...)

Writers such as Morgan McCall and Michael Lombardo (1983) believe that proficient leaders possess four (4) enduring traits:

1. Emotional stability and composure, irrespective of the prevailing situation

2. Good interpersonal skills, i.e., the ability to foster excellent interpersonal relationships, e.g., they are sensitive to the needs of other people and have the ability to persuade others to get things done, without using the power of coercion

3. The ability to admit that mistakes were made and find ways to correct them

4. The ability to acquire a wide range of knowledge and expertise.

Other leadership theories

√ *Theory X and Theory Y - Douglas McGregor (1960)*   √ *Theory of needs - David McClelland (1961)*

√ *Managerial Competency Traits - Richard Boyatziz (1982)*   √ *Leadership Attributes - John Gardner (1989)*

√ *Five -Factor Theory - Robert McCrae and Paul Costa (1999)*

A summary of situation theory

Situational theories of leadership are based on the principle that one leadership style will not be appropriate to all circumstances. Such theories focus on the behaviour which leaders should adopt when faced with different levels of competencies and commitment of subordinates.

Hersey-Blanchard Situational Theory

According to the Hersey-Blanchard theory of leadership, there are four leadership styles which can be adopted by leaders, under different circumstances:

The directing/telling leader

When subordinates exhibit lack of competence and commitment, the leader adopts a high task–low relationship approach.

The coaching/selling leader

When subordinates exhibit some level of competence and variable commitment, the leader adopts a high task–high relationship approach.

The participating/supporting leader

When subordinates exhibit high level of competencies but some variations in their commitment, the leader adopts a low task–high relationship approach.

The delegating leader

When subordinates exhibit high levels of competencies and commitment, the leader adopts a low task-low relationship approach.

Contingency theory
(HIGHER LEVEL FOCUS)

The contingency and situation theories are similar in that they both operate on the principle that there is no one best way to lead. However, the contingency theory extends beyond the behaviour which should be adopted by leaders and proposes that a leader's effectiveness is contingent upon a wide range of variables. Some of which include:

√ The leader's capability

√ The competence and motivation of subordinates

√ Availability of resources

√ Management (leaders)-employee relationship

√ Size and nature of the firm

√ Internal and external environments

√ State of technology

√ Leasership style.

A summary of Fiedler's contingency theory

Fiedler's (1922) contingency theory proposes that effective leadership, and hence, the performance of subordinates is contingent on a combination of two (2) factors.

1: Leadership style	2: Situational favourableness
√ Task oriented.	√ Leader-member relation.
√ Relationship oriented.	√ Task structure.
	√ Position power.

NOTE: According to Fiedler, the stronger the relationship between leaders and their subordinates

1. The more structured the task given.

2. The stronger the leader's position of power.

3. The greater the leader's control over subordinates.

Behavioural leadership theory
(HIGHER LEVEL FOCUS)

A summary of Blake and Mouton leadership model

The behavioural leadership model developed by Robert Blake and Jane Mouton is based on the principle that leaders are concerned with two variables:

1. **Concern for production:** The leader focuses on meeting objectives, ensuring work efficiency and increasing productivity.

2. **Concern for people:** The leader focuses on how best to motivate employees, e.g., meeting employees' needs.

These two dimensions form the basis of five leadership styles, which are represented on a managerial grid.

1. *Impoverished leadership style (Low People/Low Production):* The leader shows very little concern for subordinates, productivity and achievement of goals.

2. *Country-club leadership style (High People/Low Production):* The leader shows a high level of concern for subordinates but a low level of concern for achievement of goals and productivity.

(Contd...)

3. *Middle-of-the-road leadership style (Medium Production/Medium People):* The leader seeks compromise by trying to maintain a balance between the concern for subordinates and the achievement of goal and productivity.

4. *Produce-or-perish leadership style (High Production/Low People):* The leader focuses exclusively on achievement of goals and productivity and shows a low concern for subordinates.

5. *Team leadership style (High Production/High People):* The leader has a high level of concern for achieving goals and productivity, while maintaining the same level of concern for subordinates.

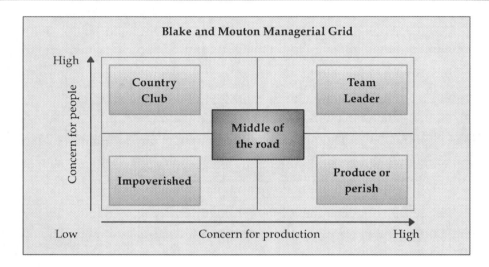

Blake and Mouton Managerial Grid

Robert Tannenbaum and Warren Schmidt continuum of leadership behaviour

The Tannenbaum and Schmidt Continuum represent the relationship between the level of freedom leaders allow their subordinates and the level of authority they choose to maintain.

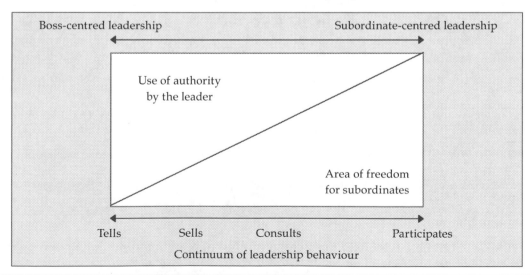

(Contd...)

The following are the levels of leadership behaviour found along the continuum, from left to right:

1. **Telling behaviour:** The leader makes all decisions, and subordinates have to accept and work with that decision.

2. **Selling behaviour:** The leader makes the decision and uses various persuasive tactics to gain subordinates' support for the decision.

3. **Consulting behaviour:** The leader makes tentative decisions and consults with subordinates on the best way forward.

4. **Participative behaviour:** The leader invites all employees to participate in the decision-making process.

NOTE: Leaders who operate at the left of the continuum are *task centred*, less *relationship-oriented* and maintain *high degree of control*, while those who operate at the right are *people-oriented* and delegate *considerable authority and responsibility to their subordinates*.

The point on the continuum at which a leader operates depends on the situation.

A summary of Likert's system of management

According to Dr. Renesis Likert, an organisation's success can be influenced by one of the four systems of management:

1. **The exploitative authoritative system**
   - √ Management makes all the decisions.
   - √ Management is task oriented but less focused on building relationships.
   - √ Management uses coercive measures to get things done.
   - √ Subordinates are expected to abide by the management's decisions.
   - √ Team building is not a focus of management.

2. **Benevolent authoritative system**
   - √ All decisions are made by the management.
   - √ Subordinates are motivated by the promise of rewards for excellence.
   - √ Limited levels of feedback are encouraged from subordinates.
   - √ Team work is encouraged on a very small scale.

3. **Consultative system**
   - √ Subordinates are involved in the decision-making process.
   - √ An open-door policy encourages subordinates to share ideas.
   - √ Managers are ultimately responsible for achieving organisational goals.
   - √ Management has total control over all decisions.

4. **Participative (group) system**
   - √ Management is more trusting of, and confident about, the abilities of subordinates.
   - √ Both management and subordinates are responsible for organisational goals.
   - √ Team work is an integral part of the organisation.
   - √ An open-door policy encourages subordinates to share ideas.
   - √ Subordinates are offered economic incentives for meeting objectives.

The differences between leadership and management
(HIGHER LEVEL FOCUS)

Leadership

√ A facet of management

√ Involves setting new directions for theorganisation – facilitating change

√ Motivates team members to work towards achieving organisational goals

√ Develops and grooms team members

Management

√ Strives for innovation and creativity

√ Conforms to set rules and procedures

√ High concern for structured relationships

√ Concerned with authority

√ Concentrates on doing what is right

You must be able to:

1. **Discuss** whether successful leadership in identified situations is the result of natural skills and abilities, or is a consequence of the circumstances faced.

2. **Apply** to given situations the theories of writers, such as Likert, Fiedler, Blake and Mouton, and Tannenbaum and Schmidt.

The functions of management
(HIGHER LEVEL FOCUS)

The key functions of management
The key functions of management can be summarised as follows:

Planning
Establishing organisational objectives and developing strategies for achieving them

Organising
Coordinating and allocating resources effectively and efficiently

Controlling
Monitoring outcomes and regulating activities to achieve objectives

Directing
Influencing and motivating members to work towards achieving objectives

Management theories

A summary of Henri Fayol's functions of management

1. **Planning:** Drawing up plans to establish goals and objectives, based on projections for the future

2. **Organising:** Ensuring the availability of structure, systems and resources required for achieving goals and objectives.

3. **Commanding:** Maintaining the activities amongst personnel – this involves leadership

4. **Coordinating:** Synchronising all management functions and appropriate resources

5. **Controlling:** Ensuring that activities and results conform to standard policies, practices and expectations.

A summary of Peter Drucker's functions of management

1. Setting clear objectives

2. Organising activities and resources

3. Communicating with and motivating subordinates

4. Outlining performance measures

5. Developing people – including those in the management

A summary of Charles Handy's functions of management

√ To provide vision.

√ To motivate and inspire.

√ To coordinate and unify.

You must be able to **explain** the key functions of management, applying the theories of writers, such as Fayol, Handy and Drucker.

© The IBO, 2007

2.5: MOTIVATION

Motivation in theory

Motivation

The individual or team
Motivation is about having the desire, drive and determination to achieve a setgoal.

The leader/manager
Motivation is about inspiring and encouraging subordinates and team members to achieve set goals.

Content theories of motivation

A summary of F.W. Taylor's theory of scientific management

F.W. Taylor proposed that workers are motivated by money and as a means of raising their motivation levels managers have to ensure the following:

1. Clear lines of authority and responsibility are established

2. Employees are properly coordinated and supervised to ensure that the task is performed in the most optimal way

3. Efficient production procedures and processes are in place

4. Responsibility for outcomes is shared between workers and management

5. Employees are provided with adequate training and tools required to complete the task

6. Employees are given opportunities to take up tasks in their areas of specialisation

7. Implementation of incentive schemes - pay by results.

A summary of Abraham Maslow's hierarchy of needs

Abraham Maslow suggested that employees have five categories of needs which must be satisfied at work. He categorised these needs under, what is known today as, *Maslow's hierarchy of needs*.

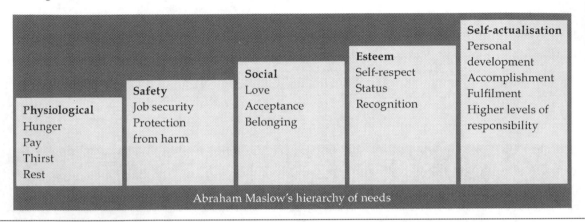

Abraham Maslow's hierarchy of needs

A summary of Douglas McGregor's Theory X and Theory Y

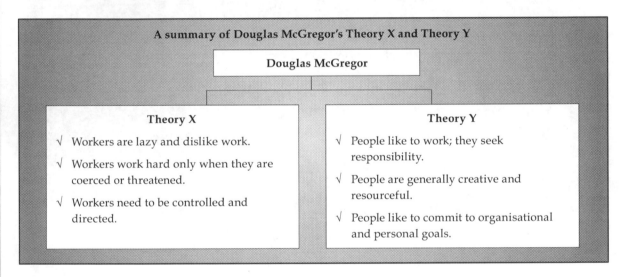

Douglas McGregor

Theory X

√ Workers are lazy and dislike work.

√ Workers work hard only when they are coerced or threatened.

√ Workers need to be controlled and directed.

Theory Y

√ People like to work; they seek responsibility.

√ People are generally creative and resourceful.

√ People like to commit to organisational and personal goals.

Summary of Hertzberg's two factors theory of motivation

Factor # 1: Hygiene factors

Management must pay attention to hygiene factors in order to prevent employees' dissatisfaction. Some of the hygiene factors (maintenance needs) are listed below:

√ Working conditions

√ Pay and other benefits

√ Quality of leadership and management

√ Organisation policies and procedures and their implementation.

√ Security

√ The organisation itself

√ Interpersonal relationships

Factor # 2: Motivation factors

Management must pay attention to these factors as they help achieve higher levels of employee motivation. Some motivators include:

√ Responsibility

√ Progression within the organisation

√ Recognition for achievement

√ Interesting/challenging job role.

According to Herzberg, work within an organisation should be organised with the following objectives:

1. Job enlargement   **2. Job rotation**   **3. Job enrichment.**

You must be able to **apply** the content theories to given situations.   © The IBO, 2007

The intrinsic and extrinsic needs which must be satisfied at work

Intrinsic needs

The desire for attaining self-actualisation within the job role, e.g., the need for fulfilment and accomplishment, job satisfaction.

Extrinsic needs

The desire for tangible or intangible rewards which are outside of the job role, e.g., financial bonuses, promotions.

Some financial and non-financial rewards that motivate individuals

Non-financial rewards

√ Certificates of recognition

√ Trophies

√ Seminars, conferences, workshops

√ Special office space

√ Empowerment

√ Promotion

√ Refreshments

Financial rewards

√ Pay increase

√ Pension plans

√ Retirement plans

√ Profit sharing

√ Performance-related incentives

√ Paid holiday trips

√ Health Insurance

You must be able to **analyse** the intrinsic and extrinsic needs that have to be satisfied at work, and the rewards (financial and non-financial) that motivate individuals.

© The IBO, 2007

Content theories of Mayo and McClelland
(HIGHER LEVEL FOCUS)

A summary of Elton Mayo's content theory

Based on the results of his famous *Hawthorne Studies*, Elton Mayo made the following conclusions about what motivates workers:

Good pay and working conditions are not the only rewards which motivate workers.

Workers are best motivated when

√ They get recognition for the work they do

√ They work together as a team

√ They receive clear directives and are able to communicate with management

√ Management shows a great deal of interest in what they do.

A summary of David McClelland's acquired-needs theory

David McClelland's acquired-needs theory is based on the principle that people's needs are acquired on the basis of their experiences. These needs can be classified as follows:

The need for achievement (n-ach): People with a need for achievement are driven by the desire to accomplish challenging goals and excellence in whatever they do. They take very little risk and require regular feedback on their performance. These people tend to work well either on their own or with individuals with the same level of need.

The need for affiliation (n-affil): People with a need for affiliation are motivated by establishing friendly relationships with others. They tend to work well in groups and do well with tasks which require a significant amount of interaction.

The need for power (n-pow): Workers with a need for power are motivated by the prospect of being influential and effective, the assumption of leadership position and the attainment of prestige. While some are motivated by the prospect of having personal power, others are motivated by the prospect of having institutional power.

You must be able to **apply** the content theories of Mayo and McClelland. © The IBO, 2007

Process theories
(HIGHER LEVEL FOCUS)

A summary of Victor Vroom's expectancy theory of motivation

The basic principle of Vroom's theory is that workers will be motivated if they believe they can attain an expected level of performance and that attainment in performance will bring them closer to their personal goal of achieving some favourable reward. Thus, the worker will assess the following:

1. The likelihood that the effort to be extended will lead to an acceptable level of performance: **Expectancy**

2. The likelihood that the successful accomplishment of the task will lead to some favourable reward: **Instrumentality**

3. The extent to which the reward is valuable/important enough to satisfy an important need: **Valence**.

Motivation = (Valence × Expectancy) (Instrumentality)

A summary of John Adams equity theory of motivation

The basic principle of Adams' equity theory is that employees are motivated when they perceive there is an adequate balance between the work they do (**inputs**) and the rewards they receive (**outputs**).

Example of inputs
Hard work
Effort & dedication
Expertise
Flexibility

$+$

Example of outputs
Financial rewards
Recognition
Job security
Promotion

Employees' perception of a fair balance between outputs and inputs results in a motivated workforce.

You must be able to:

1. **Analyse** the effects of thought process and expectations on individual motivation.

2. **Apply** theories of writers, such as Vroom and Adams.

© The IBO, 2007

MOTIVATION IN PRACTICE

Financial motivation: Methods of payment

Wages

The amount of money paid to an employee based on the number of hours worked (time-rates) or the extent/percentage of task completed (piece-rates).

Time-rates

Employees are paid based on the amount of time they spend at work.

Advantages

√ Simple to understand and easy to implement

√ Simplifies the wage-budget planning process

√ Suited to businesses that employ workers with different skill levels

√ Employees who work beyond stipulated hours are paid *over-time rates*, which are usually higher than the regular rates.

Disadvantages

√ Expensive, as any over-time, holiday or weekend work attracts a *higher-than-normal* hourly rate

√ No incentives for working harder during the stipulated hours

√ Wages must be paid irrespective of the level of productivity.

Piece-rates

Workers are paid based on an agreed rate per unit of work/task completed.

Advantages

√ Simple to understand and easy to implement

√ Offers incentives for increased efforts

√ Increases output and reduces average cost

√ Employees can regulate their earnings by adjusting the pace at which they work.

Disadvantages

√ Employers can manipulate the system to prevent employees from reaping maximum benefit.

√ Disagreements occur on what constitutes the expected level of production.

√ Employees' earnings fluctuate based on output levels.

√ Employees are more likely to focus on quantity and neglect aspects of quality.

√ Personal performance takes precedence over collaborative efforts and team work.

Salary

This is a fixed annual remuneration which is paid on a monthly basis. Unlike wages, no extra pay is earned for working overtime or on weekends/holidays.

Advantages

√ There is no need to pay employees on time- or piece-rate.

√ Employees can be paid based on their experience, qualifications and expertise.

√ Stabilises the wage budget for employers and offers financial stability (steady flow of income) to employees.

Disadvantages

√ Workers on the same scale receive the same level of compensation, irrespective of their individual productivity.

√ An employee's income is limited to the salary scale within which they are placed.

√ An employee's salary remains unchanged within a fiscal year unless the employee gets a promotion.

Commission

This relates to a payment received by an employee, e.g., sales representative) and translates to a percentage of the sales revenue generated by the employee.

Advantages

√ Commissions are incentives offered to boost performance, e.g., increase sales volume.

√ Commissions can help enhance the productivity.

√ Labour cost is controlled.

√ Employees are motivated by the freedom to control their time and earnings.

Disadvantages

√ Employees are motivated by the prospect of high earnings rather than loyalty to the company.

√ The drive for individual success limits team building and collaborative work.

Profit-Related Pay (PRP)

Profit-related pay is a scheme where the reward, e.g., a cash bonus, received by employees is directly related to the profitability of the organisation in which they are employed.

Advantages

√ Strengthens employee commitment to ensuring the success of the organisation

√ Enhances employee productivity and efficiency

√ Reduces the attrition rate and the likelihood of absenteeism

Disadvantages

√ As the reward is not linked to the performance of individuals, employees may not be motivated to work harder.

√ If the organisation does not realise a profit, the bonus is not paid, affecting employee motivation.

Performance-Related Pay (PRP)

Performance-related pay is a system that rewards workers for fully or partially achieving a set goal or standard.

Advantages

√ Motivates employees to achieve set standards/targets, as these form the basis for earning financial incentives

√ Improves productivity, efficiency and quality - standards or goals are clearly outlined

√ Helps evaluate and track individual and group performance

√ Sets clear goals for employees to work towards

Disadvantages

√ De-motivate employees if goals to be achieved are unrealistic

√ Encourages individualism and limits the benefits which can be gained from working in teams

√ Limits creativity, as employees may be tied to set goals or standards

√ Not all employees work hard for a set reward, especially if they perceive the reward to be less substantial

Employee share-ownership scheme

Employee share-ownership scheme is a system where employees are rewarded with the opportunity to purchase shares in the company.

Advantages

√ Gives employees the opportunity to have a stake in the company's growth and profitability

√ Motivates employees to take more personal interest in the company's success

√ Encourages employee retention

Disadvantages

√ Falling share prices dampen employee morale and motivation.

√ If the company fails, employees risk losing their jobs and the money invested in shares.

√ Issuing new shares decreases the value of existing shares.

Fringe payments

These are non-monetary rewards given to employees, in addition to the regular compensation they receive for the work they do. Some examples of fringe payments are listed below:

- √ Private health insurance
- √ Housing
- √ Use of company car
- √ Paid holiday trips
- √ Paid continuing education
- √ Exclusive membership to clubs and restaurants.

You must be able to:

1. **Evaluate** alternative financial reward packages

2. **Evaluate** the impact of financial reward packages on job satisfaction, motivation and productivity.

MOTIVATION IN PRACTICE

Non-financial motivation

Job enrichment (Vertical loading)

Job enrichment is the process of giving employees variety in the tasks they are assigned. It also involves giving employees some level of autonomy for planning and controlling the activities associated with their respective job functions.

The key principles of job enrichment.

 Employees must be given the autonomy, responsibility, independence and support to complete tasks which are meaningful and challenging.

 Employees must be given adequate feedback on how well they are doing, while the management should reflect on how best to improve their performance.

 Employees must be given a variety of tasks and challenges with varying levels of difficulty.

Some job-enrichment strategies

- √ Job rotation
- √ Autonomous work groups
- √ Combining job roles/functions
- √ Grouping employees into teams and specialised project units
- √ Giving employees more power and authority for making job-related decisions
- √ Encouraging suggestions and feedback – open-door policy
- √ Giving employees the leverage and resources to be creative and innovative

Some ways in which successful job-enrichment schemes affect job satisfaction, motivation and productivity

√ Eliminating the monotony associated with being confined to tasks of the same kind

√ Giving employees the opportunity to network with colleagues from different departments

√ Allowing employees to use their skills and expertise to solve challenging problems and complete challenging tasks

√ Giving employees the opportunity to acquire new skills and expertise

---

Job enlargement (Horizontal Loading)

Job enlargement increases the scope of an employee's job by increasing the number of tasks they are engaged in, e.g., a math teacher being asked to teach science in addition to their regular teaching load.

As a non-financial reward, job enlargement affects employee satisfaction, motivation and productivity as it:

√ Broadens the scope of the expected output, resulting in increased productivity

√ Frees up employees from the monotony associated with performing a single task

√ Restricts long-term motivation, as the tasks are of the same nature and offer limited challenges.

Empowerment

Empowerment is the act of giving employees the authority to make decisions, implement ideas and control the activities related to their specific jobs. Empowerment also involves giving employees access to adequate training and resources, enabling them to be effective and productive in their jobs.

As a non-financial reward, empowerment affects employee satisfaction, motivation and productivity as it:

√ Boosts employee morale and confidence

√ Allows employees to decide how best to accomplish a given task

√ Bestows employees with the responsibility of improving the processes and methodologies followed in the organisation

√ Motivates employees by the satisfaction and confidence they gain from relevant training and availability of resources to get the job done.

Teamwork

Teamwork occurs when employees work collaboratively in a group to accomplish a task.

As a non-financial reward, teamwork affects job satisfaction, motivation and productivity in a positive manner:

√ Allows team members to share their expertise and collaborate on assigned tasks

√ Enables employees to acquire new skills

√ Facilitates open communication and exchange of information and knowledge

√ Stimulates performance through team commitment and camaraderie.

(Contd...)

Team work, however, can be limited by:

√ Conflicts between members of the team

√ Incompatibility of team members.

You must be able to:

1. **Explain** how non-financial rewards can affect job satisfaction, motivation and productivity.

2. **Evaluate** alternative methods of non-financial rewards in different circumstances in the work place. **(HL Only)**

© The IBO, 2007

2.6: ORGANISATIONAL AND CORPORATE CULTURE
(HIGHER LEVEL FOCUS)

Corporate/Organisational culture represents the unique core values and beliefs, principles and operations of an organisation that are shared by and influence the behaviour of management and employees.

Factors influencing organisational culture

Some of the factors influencing organisational culture are listed below:

√ Type of employees

√ Influence of managers   √ Leadership styles

√ Nature and size of the organisation   √ Corporate objectives

√ Changes in the external environment, e.g., increasing competition, technological changes.

You must be able to **explain** the influences on organisational culture.   © The IBO, 2007

Different corporate/organisational cultures

In their work titled *Diagnosing and Changing Organisational Culture*, Kim Cameron and David Quinn (1999) describe four different organisational/corporate cultures:

√ Hierarchy   √ Clan

√ Adhocracy   √ Market.

Characteristics of the hierarchy corporate/organisational culture

√ Formalised structured policies, procedures and processes

√ Tall organisational structures

√ A boss-centred approach to management

√ The need for organisational stability and effectiveness

√ Efficiency in undertaking assigned tasks

√ Centralised decision making

Characteristics of the adhocracy corporate/organisational culture

√ Creativity and innovation at all levels

√ Individualism and decentralised decision making

√ The need to be ahead of competitors

√ Swift response to changing internal and external conditions

√ Flexible organisation structures

Characteristics of the clan corporate/organisational culture

√ An open and friendly atmosphere at work

√ Shared values and goals, loyalty and a strong sense of tradition

√ High levels of commitment from management and subordinates

√ Management is responsive to the developmental needs of workers

√ Teamwork and consensus in decision making

√ A customer-oriented approach to business decisions

Characteristics of the market corporate/organisational culture

√ Focus on goal attainment

√ Competitive behaviour amongst management and employees

√ High levels of efficiency and productivity

√ Market dominance

√ Strong and focused leadership

You must be able to **describe** different corporate/organisational cultures and analyse their effects on, for example, motivation and organisational structure.

Cultural clashes within and between organisations

Some causes of cultural clashes

Within an organisation	Between organisations
√ New leadership	√ Mergers and acquisitions
√ Diversified workforce	√ Joint ventures
√ Lack of communication	√ Outsourcing and offshoring

Cultural clashes within and between organisations: Consequences

Some of the consequences of cultural clashes within and between organisations are:

√ Misunderstandings in communication

√ De-motivated staff

√ Fall in productivity, as employees are distracted from their duties.

√ Poor corporate image

√ Absenteeism and high attrition rate

2.7: EMPLOYER AND EMPLOYEE RELATIONS
(HIGHER LEVEL FOCUS)

Negotiations/Collective bargaining

In many companies, managers must work with labour unions which are regarded as the official representative of employees. The main reason behind employees joining trade unions is the feeling that individually they have very little power to deal with the management, but when bonded together in an officially organised manner, they are in a stronger position to negotiate many issues pertaining to their jobs.

Collective bargaining is the process of negotiation between a trade union (workers' official representative) and management, in an attempt to resolve issues pertaining to workers' rights and privileges. Some examples of issues are:

√ Employee pay and other benefits   √ Training   √ Health and safety.

A collective-bargaining contract is binding on both the union and the management.

The dynamic nature of the relationship between employees, employers and their representatives

Employers' responsibilities
√ Leadership/Management
√ Wages & other fringe benefits
√ Safe work environment

Employees' responsibilities
√ Use skills, knowledge/expertise
√ Meet set targets
√ Adhere to rules and procedures

Employees' representatives (Unions)
√ Represent employees
√ Provide information to management
√ Act as a channel of communication between workers and management

Methods employed to achieve individual and group objectives

**Methods used by employees and their representatives
in pursuit of their objectives**

Negotiations/Collective bargaining: Workers or their representatives engage in a dialogue with the management, with the intention of resolving a conflict.

Go-slow: Employees slow down the pace at which they work and bring down the productivity during their regular hours of work.

Work-to-rule: Workers do no more than the minimum amount of tasks as required by their job functions.

Overtime bans: Workers refuse to work beyond their stipulated working hours.

Strike action: Work stoppage with the aim of causing considerable economic hardship for the employer.

Methods used by employers to put pressure on employees

Negotiations/Collective bargaining: Management engages workers and their representative in a dialogue, with the intention of resolving a conflict.

Public relations: Management engages in activities, e.g., press conferences, which are aimed at soliciting support for its actions and explaining its position regarding the industrial dispute.

Threat of redundancies: Management threatens the loss of jobs for some workers.

Changes of contract: Management unilaterally changes the terms of workers' employment contracts.

Closure: A unilateral decision by management to close down the business operation completely.

Lock-outs: Management refuses workers entry into the company premises until the industrial dispute is resolved.

You must be able to **examine** the methods used by employers to pressure employees.

Employer's pressure tactics: Impact on employees, their representatives and the employer

Employees	Employee representatives	Employers
√ Better working conditions	√ Prominence with workers if they are able to deal with management actions successfully	√ Resolution to the dispute
√ Disruptions to work and family life	√ Loss of membership	√ Loss of resources and production
√ Layoff – loss of job	√ Dissolution, as some management actions are targeted at breaking up trade unions	√ Possibility of dent in corporate image
√ Stress and fatigue	√ Compromises	√ May gain public/ government understanding and support
√ Loss of pay		

You must be able to **evaluate** the effects of such actions on employees, employee representatives and the employer.

© The IBO, 2007

Sources (causes) of conflict in the workplace

Some sources (causes) of conflict in the workplace

√ Poor communication	√ Cultural clashes
√ Poor management/leadership	√ Favouritism
√ Unrealistic objectives/work expectations	√ Poor work-execution
√ Incompetence	√ Poor attitudes towards work

You must be able to **identify** the sources of conflict in the workplace. © The IBO, 2007

Conflict resolution

Alternative approaches to conflict resolution

Conciliation: An attempt by a third party to unite the management and the workers' representatives (trade union) to solve an industrial dispute.

Arbitration: A process where management and workers' representatives (trade union) agree to have the dispute addressed by a judge/negotiator (an individual or group) who decides on how to resolve the conflict.

Employee participation and industrial democracy: A process where structures and procedures are in place to facilitate and support employees' involvement in the organisation's decisionmaking process.

No-strike agreement: An agreement by unions not to initiate strike actions during the tenure of a collective labour agreement.

Single-union agreement: An agreement, between management and a trade union, that the union will represent all workers in the organisation.

You must be able to **evaluate** alternative approaches to conflict resolution. © The IBO, 2007

2.8: CRISIS MANAGEMENT AND CONTINGENCY PLANNING
(HIGHER LEVEL EXTENSION)

A crisis is an unexpected, unplanned event which can disrupt the normal functions of an organisation.

The difference between crisis management and contingency planning

Crisis management means responding appropriately to situations which may disrupt any aspect of an organisation's functions.

Contingency planning is a systematic approach towards anticipating situations that could interrupt any aspect of the business and devising short- and long-term measures to deal with those situations.

You must be able to **explain** the difference between crisis management and contingency planning.

© The IBO, 2007

The costs and benefits of contingency planning

Costs

√ Contingency planning is an expensive exercise requiring coordination of resources, adequate training of employees, regular reviews and a budget dedicated to the development of an effective plan.

√ A poor attitude towards contingency planning, e.g., complacency, limits the effectiveness of the process and the plan itself.

Benefits

√ Enables collaboration across the organisation

√ Helps evolve policies and procedures for dealing with unexpected situations

√ Identifies roles and responsibilities for dealing with crisis situations

√ Assures key stakeholders that the organisation is adequately prepared to deal with a crisis situation

You must be able to **evaluate** the costs and benefits of contingency planning. © The IBO, 2007

Contingency planning: Extent of success

√ Contingency planning is based on the probability of unforeseen situations occurring.

√ There are a number of constraints to consider e.g., budget limitations, inadequacy of resources.

√ No contingency plan is *foolproof*; there will always be weaknesses in some aspects of the plan.

√ Contingency planning is limited to the extent of the management's and the employees' commitment to the process.

You must be able to **discuss** how far it is possible to plan for a crisis. © The IBO, 2007

3.1: SOURCE OF FINANCE

The need for business finance

There are two general reasons why businesses need finance.

1. **To meet capital expenditure:** Expenditure related to the acquisition of new fixed assets or improving existing fixed assets to increase their value, e.g., the purchase of a machine.

2. **To meet revenue expenditure:** Spending on items and activities which occur on a day-to-day basis, e.g., the payment of wages and salaries.

Sources of funding in the long, medium and short term

Sources	Examples	Classification
Internal sources	Retained profits	Medium term
	Personal finances	Short term
	Working capital	Short term
External sources	Shares: Preference and Ordinary	Long term
	Loans: Banks, debentures, venture capital	Short, medium, long term
	Bank overdrafts	Short term

Sources of funding and circumstances under which they are appropriate

Sources	Circumstances under which they may be appropriate
Internal sources	√ Financing revenue expenditure, e.g., working capital √ Financing short-term projects, such as increasing stock levels, e.g., retained earnings
External sources	√ Financing external expansion, e.g., Equity – shares. √ Financing payroll, e.g., bank overdraft.

NOTE: There are a number of other external and internal sources of funding, for example:

√ Debt factoring   √ Leases   √ Hire purchase

√ Trade credits   √ Mortgages   √ Sale of assets.

Each type of funding has considerable advantages and disadvantages, e.g., while personal finance may be readily available, it may not be adequate enough to finance large scale projects.

Debt vs. Equity	
Sources of debt financing √ Long-term loans √ Debentures √ Hire purchase √ Leasing	**Sources of equity financing** √ Venture capital √ Business angels √ Initial Public Offering (IPO) √ Franchising

Debt	**Equity**
√ Ownership of the firm is not diluted. √ Less complicated process. √ Interest on the debt to be paid.	√ Dilutes ownership of the firm. √ Very complicated process. √ Possible wider capital base.

Factors influencing a firm's choice of source of funding

√ Nature of the proposed investment, e.g., large or small scale project

√ Nature and size of the firm, e.g., company or partnership

√ Owner's desire to retain or relinquish control

√ Cost of borrowing, that is, the interest rate associated with borrowing the loan

Initial Public Offering (IPO)

The act of a company offering shares to the public for the first time is referred to as Initial Public Offering (IPO).

Types of share capital

Authorised share capital: The total capital the company is permitted to acquire through the issue of shares to the public.

Issued share capital: The percentage of shares from the authorised share capital which has been sold to the shareholders.

Paid-up capital: Total value of issued shares that have been paid for in full.

Types of shares

Ordinary shares: The most common form of shares where shareholders receive dividends as a return on their investment in the company. The payment of dividends, however, is subject to issues such as the profitability of the company.

Preference shares: Unlike ordinary shares, preference shares have a fixed-percentage dividend. Preference shareholders are paid dividends before ordinary shareholders.

SOURCES OF FUNDING, TYPE, APPROPRIATENESS, ADVANTAGES AND DISADVANTAGES

INTERNAL	TYPE	APPROPRIATENESS	ADVANTAGES OF USAGE	DISADVANTAGES OF USAGE
Personal Funds	Short-term	Sole Trader start-up.	Readily available. No interest charges for borrowing	Limited to small scale projects. Reduces personal asset of owners.
Working Capital	Short-term	To finance every day expenses, e.g., wages	Readily available. No interest to be paid.	Not enough to finance large scale projects. Reduce the firm's liquidity position.
Retained Profit	Short-term	Repair of fixed assets.	The firm avoids borrowing. Saves costs and time associated with applying for and repaying a loan.	Not enough to finance large scale operations. Reduces the firm's financial reserves.
EXTERNAL	**TYPE**	**APPROPRIATENESS**	**ADVANTAGES OF USAGE**	**DISADVANTAGES OF USAGE**
Overdrafts	Short-term	To purchase stock	Interest is paid only when the overdraft facility is used.	A short-term source of funding. Rate charges on overdrafts are normally over the financial institution's base rate.
Shares	Long-term	Finance expansion	Large source of funds. Additional shares can be sold to acquire follow up capital for funding expansion.	Dilutions of ownership as shareholders are part-owners of the business (company). Time consuming and costly due to the strict regulations which must be adhere to when raising share capital.
Debentures	Long-term	Finance expansion	No dilution of ownership. Large source of long-term funds.	Debenture interest must be paid even if the business makes a loss. Increases the firm's gearing ratio.
Loan Capital e.g., mortgage	Long/ Medium-Term	Finance the purchase of fixed assets	There is no dilution of ownership as the bank, for example, does not part take in a share of the profits or ownership of the firm. Provides access to cash which can be used to finance operations.	There is a financial cost (fixed or variable rate) associated with borrowing loans. The amount of loan is limited by the value of the borrower's collateral.

You must be able to:

1. Evaluate the advantages and disadvantages of each form of finance.
2. Evaluate the appropriateness of a source of finance for a given situation.

3.2: INVESTMENT APPRAISAL

Investment appraisal is a process of evaluating the attractiveness of an investment proposal. Although various methods focus on quantitative techniques, factoring qualitative considerations into the appraisal process is equally important if a decision regarding the profitability and desirability of a project is to be successful. For example, to successfully appraise the profitability and desirability of investing in a machine, the following information must be considered:

1. The initial cost of the machine

2. The estimated economic life of the machine

3. The estimated/forecasted yearly financial returns from the machine

4. The residual value (the monetary value) of the machine at the end of its estimated economic life

5. Qualitative factors, e.g., the technical specifications of the machine.

A problem

Caribbean Traders Ltd. is planning to purchase a new machine which would cost $150,000. The machine is expected to reduce: (a) the time involved in processing the wood required for making furniture and (b) the time involved in manufacturing one piece of furniture. The life expectancy of the machine is 5 years, and its forecasted yearly expected cash flows are outlined in the table below.

Year	Annual net returns ($)
0	(150,000)
1	25,000
2	40,000
3	30,000
4	55,000
5	58,000

Use the information presented in the table to calculate:

1. The payback period for this proposed investment

2. The Average Rate of Return (ARR)

3. The Net Present Value (NPV)

4. Analyse the results of your calculation.

The payback period

The payback period method appraises the likelihood of an investment recouping its initial cost within a reasonable period of time. If Caribbean Traders Ltd. invests $150,000 on the machine, it can expect to recoup this investment at the end of 4 years.

The Average Rate of Returns (ARR)

This method is used to appraise the average annual profit to be gained from the investment as a percentage of the capital invested.

$$\text{ARR} = \frac{\text{Average returns/Profit} \times 100}{\text{Capital invested}}$$

(Contd...)

For Caribbean Traders Ltd., the Average Rate of Return (ARR) is calculated using the following steps:

1. Calculate the sum of positive cash flows = $208,000

2. Subtract the capital invested in the machine from the sum of positive cash flows

$$\$208,000 - \$150,000 = \$58,000 \text{ (Profit for five years)}$$

3. Divide the profit ($58,000) by the expected life of the machine (5 years)

$$\$58,000/5 = \$11,600 \text{ (Average returns/Profit)}$$

4. Apply the ARR formula

$$ARR = \frac{\$11,600 \times 100}{\$150,000} = 7.7\%$$

Interpretation: Caribbean Traders Ltd. can expect an ARR of 7.7% per annum from its investment in the machine. However, the extent to which 7.7% returns per annum is desirable will depend on a number of factors, e.g., management's financial objectives.

Discounted Cash Flow (DCF) and Net Present Value (NPV)
(HIGHER LEVEL FOCUS)

Discounted Cash Flow is a method of appraisal used in conjunction with the NPV.

Taken by itself, DCF is used to analyse today's value of future cash flows, through the use of discount factors. If the discounted value is higher than the cost of investment, then the project, based on this analysis alone, is considered viable.

Discount factors which can be determined from standard discount-factor tables are used to calculate discount cash flows.

Net Present Value is a method of appraisal based on the fact that $1.00 today will not be worth the same in the future. In other words, NPV is about comparing the value of a sum of money today, to the value of that same sum of money in the future. Therefore, companies such as Caribbean Traders Ltd. will be keen to know the value of their financial returns, (from purchasing and operating the machine), in the future when compared with the value of the same returns today.

General rule: If the NPV is positive, the project is deemed to be profitable. Consequently, the higher the NPV, the greater is the profitability of the project.

Considering the case of Caribbean Traders Ltd., determine the Net Present Value of the investment at a discount rate of 10%.

NOTE: The discount rates are taken from the discount-factor table. Additionally, there are a number of factors which determine the rate at which the investment will be discounted. Some of these factors include:

√ The prevailing interest rates

√ Duration of the investment

√ Rate of inflation

√ Management objectives regarding the investment

√ Level of risk associated with the investment.

Year	Net returns ($)	Discount factors (10%)	Calculations	Present values
0	(150,000)	1	(150,000) x 1	(150,000)
1	25,000	0.909	25,000 x 0.909	22,725
2	40,000	0.826	40,000 x 0.826	33,040
3	30,000	0.757	30,000 x 0.757	22,710
4	55,000	0.683	55,000 x 0.683	37,565
5	58,000	0.621	58,000 x 0.621	36,018
		Total DCF/PV		152,058
Inference: The future earning from the investment is worth **$152,058** today.				

Calculating the Net Present Value

Net Present Value (NPV) = Total Discounted Cash Flows or Present Values – Initial Investment

$152,058 - $150,000 = $2,058

The NPV is positive (at **$2,058**), indicating that the project is viable.

Method of appraisal	Advantages	Disadvantages
Payback period	√ Easy to use √ Projects with slow returns can be quickly identified	√ Does not consider cash flow beyond the payback period √ Does not consider profitability
Average Rate of Return	√ Considers cash flow and profitability of investment √ Easy to understand and use	√ Does not recognise that the value of money depreciates over time √ Ignores the timing of cash flow
Net Present Value	√ Considers time value of money √ Allows for varying rates of discounts, depending on factors, such as inflation	√ Can be difficult to understand and use √ Sensitive to discount rates

Qualitative factors affecting investment decisions

√ **Political factors:** for e.g., government legislation, government stability

√ **Economic factors:** for e.g., level of inflation, unemployment/employment, and state of the economy

√ **Social factors:** for e.g., demographic trends

√ **Technological factors:** for e.g., changing technology and technological infrastructure to support investment decisions

You must be able to:

1. **Calculate** the payback period and ARR for an investment.

2. **Analyse** the results of the calculations.

3. **Calculate** the NPV for an investment and **analyse** the results of your calculation. **(HL Only)**

3.3: WORKING CAPITAL

Working capital is the life blood of a business. It is a measure of the finances a company has to meet its day-to-day expenses.

Formula: Working Capital = Current Assets – Current Liabilities

Some uses of working capital

√ Purchase stocks

√ Pay wages and salaries

√ Pay advertising costs

The working-capital cycle

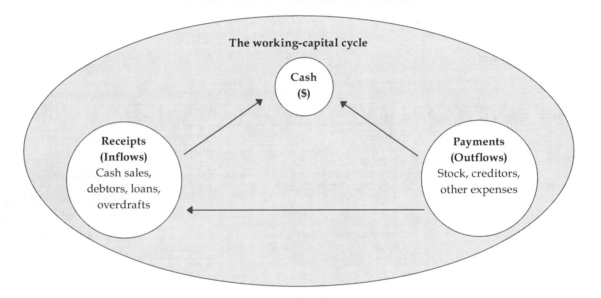

The working-capital cycle

Cash flows into the business, through sales revenue, debtor payments, loans and other financial sources (such as overdrafts).Cash flows out of the business, due to payments for stocks, creditors and other overheads.

The main components of the working-capital cycle are **stocks, debtors, creditors** and **cash** the business holds.

To maintain a healthy working-capital cycle, the business must manage **stocks, debtors, creditors** and **cash** effectively.

You must be able to **define** working capital and explain the working-capital cycle.   © The IBO, 2007

Cash flow forecasts

A cash-flow forecast is an estimate of cash coming into and going out of the business during a certain period of time. It enables the management to track and manage future income and expenditure. More importantly, it is used as a financial planning tool.

How to conduct a cash flow forecast

First step: Determine the sources of revenue/income for the month. For example, payments from debtors, cash sales, loans.

Second step: Determine the payments to be made for the month. For example, wages, payment to creditors, telephone bills.

Third step: Reconcile cash receipts with payments for the month. That is, account for opening and closing balances.

Caribbean Traders Ltd.

Cash forecast for the year 2008

Details	January ($)	February ($)	March ($)
CASH REVENUE			
Income from Sales	10,000	25,000	20,000
Income from Debtors	6,000	5,000	4,000
Total Cash Revenue	**16,000**	**30,000**	**24,000**
CASH PAYMENTS			
Employees' Wages	5,000	4,000	4,500
Utilities	4,000	2,500	6,000
Total Cash Payments	**9,000**	**6,500**	**10,500**
Net Cash Flow	7,000	23,500	13,500
Opening Balance	0	7000	30,500
Closing Balance	7,000	30,500	44,000

Although a business's trading and profit and loss account reflects profitability, it may be experiencing cashflow problems, due to a number of reasons:

√ Selling goods or rendering services on credit terms   √ Overtrading

√ Paying creditors too quickly   √ Debtors may be delaying the payment.

Also, businesses with healthy cash flows may be unprofitable, due to rising prices and increasing operational costs.

Some other reasons for drawing up a cash-flow forecast

1. As a requirement for availing a business loan
2. To identify periods when there is likely to be cash-flow problems and to take corrective measures before those problems occur

You must be able to **prepare** a cash-flow forecast from given information.   © The IBO, 2007

Some advantages and disadvantages of cash-flow forecasts

Advantages

√ Facilitate financial planning

√ Useful when trying to raise funds from external sources

Disadvantages

√ The prediction can be affected by changes in the external environment

√ Cash flow forecasts are just predictions

Managing working capital: Strategies for dealing with liquidity problems

√ Adopt a strict credit-control policy

√ Delay payments to creditors

√ Increase prices

√ Source external funding

You must be able to **evaluate** the strategies for dealing with liquidity problems. © The IBO, 2007

3.4: BUDGETING
(HIGHER LEVEL FOCUS)

A budget is a financial plan for a specific time period. It outlines how financial resources will be utilised.

Methods of budgeting

 Zero-based budgeting: Allows each department to justify the budgetary allocations it seeks for each period.

 Flexible budgeting: Allows for changes in the stipulated budgeted amounts to support changes in business activities.

Fixed budgeting: Budget remains the same, irrespective of changes in business activities.

 Incremental budgeting: Uses historical budget figures and performance as a basis for current budget allocations.

The importance of budgeting for organisations

√ Facilitates financial planning, control and coordination

√ Monitors budgetary performance standards

√ Allows for evaluation of budget outcomes

√ Motivates employees

√ Communicates financial expectations and outcomes

Some limitations of budgeting

√ Too much emphasis on results which can fall short of expectations

√ Lack of precision, as performance variances are often inevitable

√ Unrealistic budgets can lead to inefficiencies

√ The impact of qualitative factors often not considered

√ Lack of flexibility for adapting to changing conditions

Budgetary control

Budgetary control is the process of comparing the actual performance of the budget against the planned performance and implementing corrective action if necessary.

Variance analysis is a useful tool in the budgetary-control process.

You should be able to **explain** the importance of budgeting for organisations.

Variance analysis

Variance analysis is an examination of the reasons for differences between actual and expected outcomes. Variance analyses help the management to identify the causes of deviation from expected outcomes and, take corrective action where necessary.

For example, a variance in expenditure may be represented by a difference between budgeted and actual expenditure.

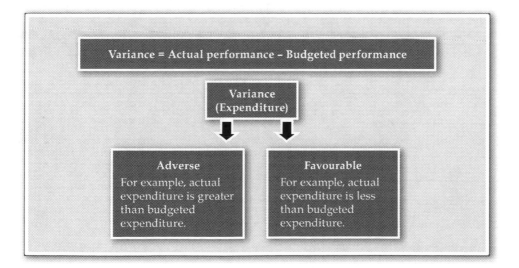

A budget statement for Caribbean Traders Ltd.

Details	Budgeted expenditure ($)	Actual expenditure ($)	Variance ($)
Direct labour	5,000	5,800	800 **(A)**
Direct material	7,000	6,500	500 **(F)**
Variable overheads	4,500	4,300	200 **(F)**
Fixed costs	8,000	8,000	0
Total costs	24,500	24,600	100 **(A)**

Once variances are identified management must determine the possible causes of the variances (adverse or favourable) and take corrective measures.

The role of budgets and variances in strategic planning

Budgets	Variances
√ Coordination and control	√ Aid budget planning and control
√ Financial planning	√ Help management to identify and address the causes of variances
√ Allocation of financial resources	
√ Communication	√ Influence management actions towards ensuring accuracy of performance
√ Motivation	
√ Evaluation	

3.5: FINAL ACCOUNTS

The purpose of accounts

√ **Communication:** Helps communicate financial information to stakeholders, e.g., shareholders, employees, investors.

√ **Planning and control:** Boosts financial planning and control.

√ **Evaluation:** Serves as the basis for evaluating the financial performance of a business.

√ **Allocation of resources:** Provides information on the allocation of monetary resources within the business.

√ **Fraud detection:** Helps detect the misuse of funds.

Accounts for Limited Companies

Caribbean Traders Ltd.

Trading and Profit and Loss and Appropriation Account for year ended 31 December, 2007

	$	$
Sales revenue		455,000
Less cost of sales/Goods sold		
Opening stock	15,000	
Add purchases	100,000	
	115,000	
Less closing stock	5000	
Cost of sales		110,000
Gross profit		**345,000**
Less Expenses		
Rent	10,000	
Utilities	6,000	
Wages	100,000	
Directors' remuneration	55,000	
		171,000
Operating profit		**174,000**
Add non-operating income		10,000
Net profit before interest and tax		**184,000**
Less interest		40,000
Net profit		144,000
Less taxes		45,000
Net profit after interest and tax		99,000
Less proposed dividends		48,500
Retained earnings		50,500

> Trading account: In this section the gross profit/loss resulting from trading activities is calculated.

> **Profit and loss account:** In this section net profit/loss which is generated after all expenses have been paid is calculated.

> **Appropriation account:** This section shows how the net profit is distributed among taxes, interest, dividends and retained earnings.

Income statement terminologies

In the trading account
Gross Profit is calculated here

Sales revenue
Income generated from sales
Sales Revenue = Price X Quantity Sold

Cost of Goods Sold (COGS)
The direct costs associated with the sale of goods
COGS= Opening stock + New purchases – Closing stock

Strategies for improving gross profit

√ Increasing the price of goods/services

√ Sourcing and using cheaper suppliers

Gross profit/loss: The sales revenue exceeds the cost of goods sold.
Gross Profit = Sales Revenue – Cost of Goods Sold

In the profit and loss account
Net Profit is calculated here

Net profit/loss: Excess of gross profit after expenses are deducted.
Net Profit = Gross Profit - Expenses

Net profit can be improved by:

Employing strategies to reduce expenses, e.g., monitoring the use of electricity in an office building.

Income generated from non-core (operating) activities must be added to the net profit before it is brought down to the appropriation account. Commission received is an example of income from non-operating activities.

In the appropriation account
The net profit is distributed here

Interest: A percentage of the net profit is allocated for paying interest on, e.g., loans.

Corporation tax: By legislation, companies must pay a certain percentage of their net earnings as corporate tax.

Dividends: A percentage of the net profit is set aside for paying dividends to the shareholders of the company.

Retained profit: This represents net profit which remains after taxes and dividends have been paid. It must be transferred to the balance sheet.

The balance sheet

The balance sheet is a financial statement which shows the assets, liabilities, and financial structure of the business at a specific time.

Caribbean Traders Ltd.
Balance Sheet as at 31 December, 2007

Fixed assets	$	$	$
Buildings			5,00,000
Equipment			150,000
Motor vehicle			80,000
			730,000
Current assets			
Stock		5,000	
Debtors		10,000	
Cash at bank		200,000	
Cash in hand		50,000	
		265,000	
Less current liabilities			
Creditors	5000		
Overdraft (short-term loan)	8,000		
Corporation tax	45,000		
Proposed dividends	48,500		
		106,500	
Working capital (Net current asset)			158,500
Total net asset			888,500
Financed by:			
Long-term liabilities		31,000	
Capital & reserves:			
Share capital		782,500	
Reserve		24,500	
Retained earnings/profit		50,500	
Capital employed			888,500

Fixed assets: Assets which are generally not acquired for resale and are used by the firm for a number of years, e.g., land, buildings, vehicles, Mplant, machinery.

Current assets: Assets which are liquidated or used up within the accounting period. They include stock, debtors, cash in the bank, and cash held by the firm. The value of a firm's current assets must be adequate enough to support its current liabilities.

Net current assets: This is also known as working capital and represents the ability of the firm to meet its day-today expenses.

Net asset: This is a sum of total fixed assets and net current assets.

Current liabilities: These represent the debts which must be paid within the accounting period, i.e., one year. They include debts to suppliers, proposed dividends, taxes and shortterm loans.

Long-term liabilities: These represent debts which are to be current assets.paid in more than one year. They are used to fund capital projects. Examples of long-term liabilities include debentures and long-term bank loans.

Capital and reserves: Share capital, reserves and retained profit. The sum of these three balance-sheet items is referred to as *capital employed or shareholders' funds.*

You should be able to **construct** and **amend** accounts from given information.　　　© The IBO, 2007

Advantages and limitations of the final accounts

The trading and profit and loss account

Advantages

√ Helps measure a firm's profitability

√ Helps a firm determine (1) its earnings per share and (2) its efficiency in selling stocks and managing debtors and creditors

√ Facilitates financial planning. For example, it helps identify expenses which may need to be reduced during the next accounting period

√ Enables comparisons between current and past financial performances

Limitations

√ Overlooks the qualitative influences on profit

√ Can be manipulated to reflect the management's desired outcome; and mislead stakeholders

√ Provides only a historical view of a business' financial position

The balance sheet

Advantages

√ Helps determine the growth or decline of the business' net worth.

√ Helps ascertain the value of assets and liabilities of the business at a specific time.

√ Enables potential lenders to assess the financial merit of the business.

√ Helps determine how the business operation is financed.

Limitations

√ The balance sheet alone is not enough to assess a firm's financial status. It must be analysed in conjunction with income and cash-flow statements.

√ Does not reflect the financial value of intangible assets, e.g., goodwill

√ Can be manipulated to reflect an outcome which does not represent the firm's actual financial status

√ Does not consider non-financial factors and their effects on fixed assets, shares and other elements in the balance sheet

√ The value of fixed assets depends on the method of depreciation used

The importance of final accounts to stakeholder groups

Various stakeholder groups will have an interest in the financial status of the firm, and each group will be specifically interested in one or more aspects of the final accounts.

Stakeholder group	Interest in the final accounts
Shareholders	√ Profitability √ Positive returns on their investment √ Capital growth √ Earnings and dividends per share
Banks and financial institutions	√ Level of gearing √ Status of assets used as collateral √ Level of investment by the company
Creditors	√ Level of debtors and creditors √ Level of working capital √ Efficiency in paying debts
Directors and managers	√ Efficiency √ Liquidity √ Profitability
Potential investors	√ Profitability √ Earnings per share √ Capital growth √ Dividend per share √ Price earning ratio

You must be able to **evaluate** the importance of final accounts to each stakeholder group.

© The IBO, 2007

Depreciation
(HIGHER LEVEL FOCUS)

Depreciation refers to a decline in value of a fixed asset over time, due to factors such as physical deterioration, age or obsolescence. *In the trading and profit and loss account, depreciation is treated as an expense, while in the balance sheet, annual depreciation of a fixed asset is subtracted from the cost of the asset.*

Methods of depreciation

Straight-line method

This method depreciates the value of an asset by an equal amount for each year of its useful life.

Reducing-balance method

Asset is depreciated by a fixed percentage; however, the depreciation percentage is higher in the initial years of its useful life.

Question

Caribbean Traders Ltd. bought a machine for $150,000. The company estimates that the machine will be in use for five (5) years after which it will be sold in scrap for $10,000. The company also assumes that the machine will be depreciated by 30% per annum, on the reducing balance.

Use the straight line and reducing-balance methods to calculate by how much the machine will depreciate over the course of its useful life and its true book value after five (5) years.

To determine the annual depreciation, using the straight-line method, use this formula:

$$\frac{\text{Original value of asset (Cost)} - \text{Estimated disposal value}}{\text{Expected useful life}}$$

$$\frac{\$150,000 - \$10,000 = \$140,000/5 = \$28,000}{5 \text{ years}}$$

Interpretation: Using the straight-line method, the lathe will be depreciated by $28,000 per year.

Year	Straight-line method		Reducing-balance method	
	Annual depreciation ($)	Net book value ($)	Annual depreciation ($)	Net book value ($)
1	150,000 – 28,000	122,000	150,000 – 45,000	105,000
2	122,000 – 28,000	94,000	105,000 - 31,500	73,500
3	94,000 – 28,000	66,000	73,500 – 22,050	51,450
4	66,000 – 28,000	38,000	51,450 – 15,435	36,015
5	38,000 – 28,000	10,000	36,015 – 10,805	25,210
	Scrap Value	10,000	Scrap Value	25,210

You must be able to **calculate** depreciation using straight-line and reducing-balance methods. © The IBO, 2007

The strengths and weaknesses of each method of depreciation

Straight-line method

Strengths

√ Simple and most commonly used

√ Same level of depreciation every year

Weakness

√ Does not consider the interest paid on fixed assets

Reducing-balance method

Strengths

√ Tax advantage

√ Asset can be sold for a higher value

Weakness

√ More complicated to calculate

You must be able to **evaluate** the strengths and weaknesses of both methods of depreciation. © The IBO, 2007

Intangible assets
(HIGHER LEVEL EXTENSION)

Intangible assets are resources of the business which are not physical in nature and are valuable to a firm's overall performance.

Asset	Meaning	Value to the firm
Goodwill	Intangible asset of a firm which results from its reputable name, products, services, employees, practices and favourable location.	Competitive advantage Customer loyalty Increase the firm's value
Patents	Give inventors legal rights to their inventions.	
Copyrights	Give, e.g., writers and artists legal protection against the unauthorised use of their work.	
Brands/Trademarks	Distinguish a firm's products or services from those of its competitors. Brands/Trademarks are protected by copyright laws.	

You must be able to **explain** the meaning and **value** to the firm of different intangible assets.

© The IBO, 2007

The difficulties associated with valuing intangible assets

Intangible assets are critical for the success of firms. However, the nature of these assets makes it difficulty to assign consistent financial values to them and as such they are often precluded from being recorded in the firm's balance sheet.

You must be able to **demonstrate an understanding** of the difficulties associated with valuing intangible assets.

© The IBO, 2007

Stock valuation
(HIGHER LEVEL FOCUS)

The stock a business holds is valued for a number of reasons, the following being the most important:

√ To determine the value of the stock coming into, being processed, or leaving the business

√ For use in the trading and profit and loss account and the balance sheet.

The stocks held by a business can be in the following forms:

1. Finished goods
2. Work-in-progress
3. Raw materials.

Methods of stock valuation

Last-In-First-Out (LIFO)

The stock which is produced or purchased last is issued or sold first.

Implications

√ Value of cost of goods sold is based on the cost of the last set of stocks purchased.

√ Value of stock in inventory is based on the cost of first set of stock purchased.

√ During an inflationary period, using LIFO for inventory valuation results in a high value for cost of goods sold and a low net profit.

√ Increase in cash flow, due to significant tax savings.

Calculations using the LIFO method

Date	Stock purchased	To be issued	Value of stocks issued	Balance at end of period	
September	50 @ $20 per unit	None	None	50 @ $20 per unit	$1000
October	40 @ $25 per unit	40 units	40 units @ $25 per unit	50 @ $20 per unit	$1000
November	Nil	40 units	40 units @ $20 per unit	10 @ $20 per unit	$ 200
December	35 @ $30 per unit	15 units	15 units @ $ 30 per unit	10 @ $20 per unit	$ 200
				20 @ $30 per unit	$ 600
	The value of closing stock at December 31st				**$ 800**

First–In–First-Out (FIFO)

The stock which is produced or purchased first is issued or sold first.

Implications

√ Value of cost of goods sold is based on the cost of the stock purchased first.

√ Value of stock in inventory is based on the cost of the last set of stock brought into the firm.

√ During an inflationary period, using FIFO for inventory valuation results in a low value for cost of goods sold and a high net profit.

√ The firm may pay higher taxes.

Date	Stock purchased	To be issued	Value of stocks issued	Balance at end of period
September	50 @ $20 per unit	None	None	50 @ $20 per unit = $1,000
October	40 @ $25 per unit	40 units	40 @ $20.00 per unit	10 @ $20 per unit = $ 200 } 40 @ $25 per unit = $1,000 } **$1,200**
November	Nil	40 units	10 @ $20 per unit 30 @ $25 per unit	10 @ $25 per unit = $ 250
December	35 @ $30 per unit	15 units	10 @ $25 per unit 5 @ $30 per unit	30 @ $30 per unit = $ 900
	The value of closing stock at December 31st			**$ 900**

You must be able to make **calculations** of closing stock using LIFO and FIFO   © The IBO, 2007

Calculating the effects of different stock valuations on profit

Assuming that 95 units were sold at $40.00 each, **sales revenue** = $3,800.

Caribbean Traders trading account for year ended 31st December 2007

	LIFO	FIFO
Sales	3,800	3,800
Purchases	3,050	3,050
Less closing stock	800	900
Cost of goods sold	2,250	2,150
Gross profit	**1,550**	**1,650**

You must be able to **calculate** the effect of different stock valuations on profit.   © The IBO, 2007

3.6: RATIO ANALYSIS

Ratio analysis uses the numbers in the trading and profit and loss account and the balance sheet to compare and assess the financial performance of a firm with regard to its profitability, liquidity, efficiency, gearing and the returns it generates on shareholders' investments.

Categories of financial ratios

√ **Profitability ratios:** measure the relative success of a firm at generating profit. They can also be described as measures of profit for each dollar of sales revenue.

√ **Liquidity ratios:** measure the ability of the firm to generate cash to pay its short-term debts.

√ **Efficiency ratios:** are used to evaluate how well the firm manages available resources/assets.

√ **Shareholder ratios:** measure the returns to shareholders in terms of their share of stock. They focus on the interest of current and future shareholders in terms of their desire for capital gains or annual dividends.

√ **Gearing ratio:** measure the extent to which a company's operation is financed by loan capital versus equity funds. The higher the level of gearing, the greater is the financial risk associated with the company.

Profitability ratios

1. **Gross Profit Margin:** A measure of gross profit as a percentage of sales revenue.

Formula: Gross Profit Margin = (Gross Profit ÷ Sales Revenue) X 100

Example: Focus on Caribbean Traders Ltd.

Gross Profit Margin = $\frac{345,000 \times 100}{455,000}$ = 76%

Interpretation: For every $100 of sales revenue, the company generates $76 in gross profit.

(Contd...)

2. **Net Profit Margin:** A measure of net profit as a percentage of sale revenue.

   Formula: Net Profit Margin = (Net Profit before interest and tax ÷ Sales Revenue) X 100

   Example: Focus on Caribbean Traders Ltd.

   $$\textbf{Net Profit Margin} = \frac{184{,}000 \times 100}{455{,}000} = 40.4\%$$

Interpretation: For every $100 of sale, the company generates $40.40 net profit.

Liquidity ratios

1. **Current Ratio:** Measures the ratio of a firm's current assets to its current liabilities.

   Formula: Current Ratio = Current Assets ÷ Current Liabilities

   Example: Focus on Caribbean Traders Ltd.

   $$\textbf{Current Ratio} = \frac{265{,}000}{106{,}500} = 2.5 \text{ times}$$

Interpretation: For every $1 of current liabilities (short-term debts) the company has $2.50 of current assets.

NOTE: A ratio of 1.5 – 2 indicates that the firm's current asset is sufficient (liquidity) to pay its shortterm debts. A Current Ratio of over 2 may be a cause for concern, as it indicates that a considerable amount of funds is tied up in current assets, e.g., stock, debtors and money in the bank.

2. **Acid Test:** A stricter test of liquidity which excludes the value of closing stock from the calculations.

   Formula: Acid Test Ratio = (Current Assets – Stock) ÷ Current Liabilities

   Example: Focus on Caribbean Traders Ltd.

   $$\textbf{Acid Test Ratio} = \frac{260{,}000}{106{,}000} = 2.4 \text{ times}$$

Interpretation: For every $1 of current liabilities the company has $2.40 of current assets. This also indicates that the company's most liquid assets (debtors, cash in hand and cash in the bank) are sufficient to satisfy its short-term debts.

NOTE: An acid test ratio of 1:1 is the most desirable liquidity position.

Efficiency ratios

1. **Stock Turnover:** Ratio of cost of good sold over average stock. It measures how many times on average within the accounting period stock of goods was sold and replenished.

   Formula: Stock turnover = Cost of goods sold ÷ Average stock*

   Example: Focus on Caribbean Traders Ltd.

   $$\textbf{Stock Turnover} = \frac{110{,}000}{10{,}000} = 11 \text{ times}$$

   $$*\text{Average stock} = \frac{(\text{Opening stock + Closing stock})}{2}$$

Interpretation: On average the company sells and replenishes its inventory (stock) 11 times a year.

(Contd…)

2. **Return on Capital Employed (ROCE):** A measure of the percentage return on capital invested in the business. It is also a measure of profitability..

Formula: ROCE = (Net profit before interest and tax ÷ Total capital employed) X 100

Example: Focus on Caribbean Traders Ltd.

$$\textbf{ROCE} = \frac{184,000 \text{ X } 100}{888,500} = 20.7\%$$

Interpretation: For every $100 of capital invested in long-term capital the company has earned a return (profit) of $20.70.

NOTE:

√ People invest in businesses with the expectation of receiving adequate returns on their investments. The higher the percentage of ROCE the more profitable the capital invested.

√ To be worthwhile, the returns generated must be higher than the prevailing interest rate (returns) on offer by banks or other forms of investments.

Efficiency ratios

(HIGHER LEVEL FOCUS)

3. **Debtor day's ratio:** A measure of how long, on average, it takes the firm to collect payments from its customers.

Formula: Debtor days = (Debtors ÷ Sales revenue) X 365

Example: Focus on Caribbean Traders Ltd.

$$\textbf{Debtor days} = \frac{10,000 \text{ X } 365}{455,000} = 8 \text{ days}$$

Interpretation: On average, the company takes 8 days to secure payment from its customers.

NOTE: Excessive debtor days, for example, beyond a standard 30 days credit to customers, would indicate the need to institute measures to manage debtors more effectively, for example, giving discounts for prompt payments.

4. **Creditor day's ratio:** A measure of how long, on average, it takes the business to pay its suppliers (creditors).

Formula: Creditor days = (Creditors ÷ Purchases) X 365

Example: Focus on Caribbean Traders Ltd.

$$\textbf{Creditor days} = \frac{5000 \text{ X } 365}{100,000} = 18 \text{ days}$$

Interpretation: On average, the company takes 18.25 days to pay its creditors.

NOTE: When a firm's financial statement reflects a ratio of more than the standard credit period (30 days for some businesses) this could be sending a number of signals about its financial position and activities, some of which include:

√ Liquidity problems, e.g., longer debtor days than usual, slower than usual stock turnover

√ Delaying payments to accommodate a short-term investment.

Shareholder ratios
(HIGHER LEVEL FOCUS)

1. **Earnings per Share (EPS):** This represents the returns per ordinary share of stock after tax.

Formula: Earning per share = (Net profit after interest and tax ÷ No. of ordinary shares)

Suppose the number of ordinary shares issued by the company is 40,000.

Example: Focus on Caribbean Traders Ltd.

$$\textbf{Earnings per Share} = \frac{99,000}{40,000} = \$2.5$$

Interpretation: The income (dividend) earned per share is $2.50. Generally, high earnings per share increase the value per share.

2. **Dividend Yield:** This measures the return per share relative to its market price.

Formula: Dividend Yield = (Annual dividend per share ÷ Market price per share) X 100

Example: Focus on Caribbean Traders Ltd.

Suppose the stock of Caribbean Traders Ltd is trading (market price per share) at $150.00 and it pays an annual dividends of $50.00 per share then:

$$\textbf{Dividend Yield} = \frac{50.00}{150.00} \times 100 = 33\%$$

NOTE:

√ This return (33%) can then be used by Caribbean Traders Ltd as a comparison with dividend yields from similar companies or its previous performance.

√ Quality, well-established companies with strong growth in their earnings tend to have higher dividend yield. However, a low dividend yield does not necessarily mean that the company has not been effective at securing adequate returns for its shareholders.

Gearing: This is a measure of the extent to which capital employed is financed by long-term loans (borrowing). The higher the level of gearing, the greater is the risk associated with the company.

Formula: Gearing = (Loan Capital ÷ Total Capital Employed) X 100

Example: Focus on Caribbean Traders Ltd.

$$\textbf{Gearing} = \frac{31,000}{888,500} \times 100 = 3.5\%$$

Interpretation: 3.5 % of capital invested comes from long-term loans (borrowing). The extent to which this is an acceptable level of gearing for the company will depend on factors such as:

√ The company's profitability

√ Size of the business

√ Interest rate at which the loan has been acquired

√ Corporate objectives, e.g., the need for growth/expansion.

√ Nature of the business

√ State of the economy

Stakeholders and their interests in financial ratios

Directors/Managers

√ To analyse the firms performance in the areas of profitability, liquidity, efficiency and returns to shareholders

√ To make decisions and control financial outcomes

√ To compare current with historical performance

√ To compare financial performance with similar businesses in the industry

Shareholders and employees

√ Profitability

√ Positive returns on their investment

√ Capital growth

√ Earnings and dividends per share

Banks and other financial institutions

√ Level of gearing

√ Status of assets used as collateral

√ Level of investment by the company

Potential investors

√ Profitability   √ Dividend per share

√ Earnings per share   √ Price earning ratio

√ Capital growth

Creditors

√ Profitability   √ Creditor days

√ Debtor days   √ Gearing

Limitations of ratio analysis

√ Accounting figures can be manipulated (window dressed) to show a stronger financial position rather than reflect the true financial position.

√ Ratio analysis is based on historical figures and does not reflect current economic values.

√ Ratio analysis does not consider the non-financial factors which can affect financial measures; hence, they cannot be interpreted in isolation.

√ Ratios cannot be used to make comparisons between firms in different industries.

Some financial and non-financial strategies to improve the value of ratios

(HIGHER LEVEL FOCUS)

Profitability Ratios

Gross Profit and Net Profit Margins

√ Increase selling prices – Increase Sales Revenue

√ Reduce selling prices – Increase Sales Revenue

√ Improved/more advertising and promotion

√ Obtain trade discounts – Reduce Cost of Sales

√ Source cheaper supplier/s – Reduce Cost of Sales

√ Reduce direct expenses – Reduce Cost of Sales

√ Improve labour efficiency – Reduce Labour Cost

√ Reduce overheads, e.g. insurance, rent, utility costs, telephone bills

√ Offshoring/sub-contracting business activities

Liquidity Ratios

Current and Acid Test Ratios

√ Reduce overhead costs, e.g., decreasing indirect expenses.

√ Monitor debtors by adopting appropriate debtor management strategies, e.g. offering discounts for prompt payments, reducing the credit period, checking credit ratings of new customers, insisting on cash on delivery for difficult customers.

√ Delay payments to creditors.

√ Negotiate better payment terms with creditors.

√ Assess the likelihood of increasing prices to increase profitability.

√ Assess the likelihood of decreasing prices to reduce stock levels and improve cash flow.

√ Transfer excess cash to an interest bearing account and then back to operating account when it is needed.

Efficiency Ratios

Stock Turnover

√ Increasing demand for products, e.g. through improved customer relations

√ Improved supply chain management, e.g. reduce lead times

√ Dispose of slow moving stocks by offering discounts and other forms of promotions

√ Improve/better demand forecasting

√ Institute a purchase/manufacture on demand system

√ Adopt a Just-in-Time production system

Efficiency Ratios

Return on Capital Employed (ROCE)

√ Improve profit margins by reducing cost

√ Reduce borrowing

√ Source cheaper suppliers

√ Expand capital base through new issue of shares

Generally, any strategy to improve profitability will contribute to improving ROCE.

Efficiency Ratios

Consider the strategies for managing debtors. For example:

√ Offer incentives for prompt payments

√ Adopt cash on delivery policy

√ Follow up on debtors whose payments are late by sending them reminder notices

√ Develop, communicate and institute clear credit policies

√ Check credit worthiness of customers who seek credit

√ Charge interest on overdue accounts

√ Threaten/take legal action.

Creditor Days Ratio

Consider the strategies for managing debtors. For example:

√ Negotiate longer credit period without penalties

√ Consider whether goodwill with creditors can be lost for late payments

√ Establish good credit ratings with suppliers.

Shareholders Ratios

Earnings per Share and Dividend Yield

The shareholder's ratios of a company can be enhanced by improving the company's overall financial position. Therefore, improvements in earnings per share and dividend yield will result from strategies that are geared towards maintaining high and sustainable returns. Such strategies are tied to the company's profitability, liquidity and efficiency positions. For example:

√ Good customer relationship

√ Focused marketing strategies

√ Effective risk management

√ Engaging CSR Initiatives

√ Efficient and effective use of resources

√ Corporate vision and purpose.

Gearing Ratio

√ Reduce long-term borrowing

√ Fund operations by increasing the issue of shares – increase capital employed

---

You must be able to **evaluate** financial and other strategies to improve the value of ratios.   © The IBO, 2007

4.1: THE ROLE OF MARKETING

A market is a place (physical location, online, telephone) where business owners or their representatives and customers engage in commercial activities. Some types of markets in which firms operate are:

√ Financial markets, e.g., the stock market

√ Industrial markets

√ Consumer markets

√ Property markets.

The market in which a firm is immersed can be characterised by a single or combination of the following factors:

√ The size of the market

√ The rate at which the market is growing

√ The firm's relative share of the market.

Market size	This is a measure of the total value or volume of sales in the market. Market size is determined by factors such as: √ The number of customers in the market √ The nature of the industry √ The nature of the goods and services available to customers.
Market growth	This is a measure of the rate at which the total sales volume in the market increases or decreases. Market growth is determined by factors such as: √ Firms' ability to attract new customers √ Firms' ability to encourage existing customers to buy more of their products √ The price at which the product is sold.
Market share Market share = $\dfrac{\text{Sales} \times 100}{\text{total}}$	This is a measure of the percentage of sales held by the firm in the market. A firm can increase its market share by: √ Implementing appropriate pricing strategies, e.g., penetration pricing √ Increasing the channels of distribution √ Adopting better advertising and promotional strategies √ Imparting appropriate training to employees.

You must be able to:

1. **Examine** the characteristics of the market in which the firm is immersed.

2. **Calculate** market share from given information.

© The IBO, 2007

Definition and nature of marketing

Definitions

"Marketing is the social process by which individuals and groups obtain what they need and want through creating and exchanging products and value with others."

Philip Kotler (1980)

"Marketing is the management process that identifies, anticipates and satisfies customer requirements profitably."

The Chartered Institute of Marketing

The nature of marketing

From the definitions we can make the following conclusions about marketing.

1. Marketing involves interaction between the representatives of businesses and their customers.

2. Marketing adds value to products and services.

3. Marketing creates value for stakeholders.

4. Marketing involves planning, executing, controlling and evaluating activities and outcomes which are geared towards satisfying customers.

5. Marketing integrates all functions of business.

6. Marketing is sometimes driven by profit.

The relationship between marketing and other business activities

MARKETING

⇨ **Production:** Production, research and development, quality control

⇨ **Finance:** Financial management and control: budgeting, receipts and payments, invoicing

⇨ **Human Resources:** Recruitment, training, wages and other forms of remuneration, redundancy arrangements

You must be able to **define** marketing and describe its relationship with other business activities.

© The IBO, 2007

Market and product orientation

Market orientation

The market-oriented firm:

√ Leverages market research to determine customers requirements

√ Produces goods and services that satisfy customer requirements.

Advantage: Through extensive research, businesses understands the needs of current and future customers. Hence, they can assess their abilities to offer goods or services which meet customer requirements.

Disadvantage: A firm may not be able to meet all the expectations of its customers.

Product orientation

The product-oriented firm:

√ Leverages product research, development and innovation

√ Focuses on the product rather than on customer requirements

√ Aims for efficiency in production, rather than meeting the requirements of a specific segment of the market.

Advantages: Innovation, research and development, quality control.

Disadvantage: Product-oriented firms are highly inflexible and are often unable to, or take a long time to, respond to changing market trends.

You must be able to **describe** the difference between market and product orientation.   © The IBO, 2007

Additional market orientations
(HIGHER LEVEL FOCUS)

1. Social Marketing

"**Social marketing** is the application of commercial marketing concepts and tools to programmes designed to influence the voluntary behaviour of target audiences where the primary objective is to improve the welfare of the target audiences and/or the society of which they are a part".

Andresen (1994)

Some features of social marketing

√ Organised around the 4Ps (Product, Price, Promotion, and Place) which drive the marketing practice of commercial firms

√ Continuous market research and evaluation are crucial to success

√ Aimed at changing people's perceptions, behaviour, attitudes and lifestyles

√ Effective communication is crucial to the success of any social-marketing effort

√ Adopted by firms in both private and public sectors. However, non-profit organisations are mostly engaged in social marketing.

√ Provides the impetus for collaboration between organisations in private and public sectors.

NOTE: Some for-profit organisations, through their Corporate Social Responsibility initiatives, are engaged in social marketing as they are aware that customers are increasingly supporting organisations that do more for the wider society.

2. Asset-led marketing

Asset-led marketing is an approach whereby a business uses its strengths, e.g., reputation, brand name, strong financial status, to promote and sell a product or service. For example, Microsoft, one of the world's largest software companies has combined its principal strength - brand name, with the needs of specific target groups to sell its Windows software.

Asset-led marketing reflects a combination of market and product-oriented approaches.

Advantages

√ Decisions are based on current and future requirements and the strength of the firm.

√ As the firm can leverage its principal strengths to remain dominant in existing markets or penetrate new markets, its profits may increase.

√ Risk-averse firms can avoid entering into a market where they may not be able to excel.

Disadvantages

√ Does not guarantee the success of a product or service

√ Limits the firms which do not intend to consider activities beyond their core competency, yet these activities may offer considerable opportunities for growth.

You must be able to **analyse** the influence of marketing orientation on the success or failure of firms.

© The IBO, 2007

Marketing goods and services

The 8Ps of marketing services

Product: Type, quality, features, brand

Price: Payment terms, discounts

Promotion: Advertising, sales promotion, public relations

Place: Location, channels of distribution, storage

The 4Ps of marketing goods

Product: Type, quality, features, brand, packaging

Price: Payment terms, discounts

Promotion: Advertising, sales promotion, public relations

Place: Location, channels of distribution, storage

People: Attitude, approachability, appearance, initiative, efficiency, skills, experience

Process: Procedures to ensure and support the efficiency of the firm's operation

Physical evidence: Appearance of the external and internal environments in which the services are rendered

Packaging: Colour, labels, materials, products/services combination

You must be able to **explain** the difference between marketing of goods and services.   © The IBO, 2007

Marketing in non-profit organisations

The marketing techniques adopted by non-profit organisations are aimed at:

√ Gaining financial and non-financial support for their activities

√ Convincing current and future customers about the benefits of their products and services.

Some marketing techniques adopted by non-profit organisations are:

√ **Communication:** Non-profit organisations must communicate their goals, objectives, strategies and results to their current and potential customers, on a continuous basis

√ **Partnerships and alliances:** Non-profit organisations must seek to align themselves with government agencies and for-profit organisations from which they can gain financial and non-financial support

√ **Identity:** A non-profit organisation must identify itself with a specific cause or project; aligning with a specific cause helps the organisation establish brand identity within the community

√ **Technology:** Like organisations in the private sector, non-profit organisations are driven by the need to expand their markets. The Internet, radio and television are some of the major media through which non-profit organisations promote their products and services

√ **Pricing:** The prices of a non-profit organisation's products and services must be well within the reach of its current and potential customers.

You must be able to **analyse** the marketing techniques of non-profit organisations.   © The IBO, 2007

A marketing plan

A marketing plan is a comprehensive document **which outlines** how a business intends to market its products and/or services. The plan focuses on issues such as:

√ Products/services to be offered

√ Current and potential customer base

√ Level and intensity of competition in the market

√ Pricing strategies

√ Financial implications

√ The marketing plan is an integral part of the overall business plan.

The elements of a marketing plan

A marketing plan includes the following elements:

1. Analysis and assessment of the firm's current position
2. Marketing budget
3. Analysis of the current market situation
4. The firm's marketing objectives
5. Analysis of competition in the market
6. Marketing strategies to be employed, e.g., pricing strategies

---

Some benefits of a marketing plan

√ Establishes and communicates the firm's marketing goals and objectives.

√ Motivates sales teams and support staff towards achieving set targets.

√ Helps identify and allocate resources to support the firm's marketing efforts.

4.2: MARKETING PLANNING

Marketing planning involves developing long and short-term strategies for effectively marketing goods/services. Effective marketing planning helps a firm to:

1. Identify its position in the market, relative to the position of its competitors

2. Outline its marketing objectives

3. Develop its marketing mix

4. Identify the most responsive and lucrative segments of the market

5. Allocate resources to specific marketing activities

6. Develop appropriate marketing strategies

7. Respond in a timely manner to changes within the market

8. Monitor performance.

The marketing mix

To successfully market goods/services, businesses must effectively combine a number of variables to generate a desired marketing outcome. The marketing mix is used to develop marketing strategies for products/services meant for a specific segment of the market.

Traditionally, the market mix is about the effective combination of 4Ps

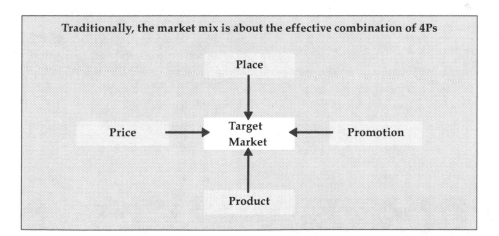

The 8Ps of marketing

Marketing experts, however, believe that to effectively market products and services, businesses must move beyond the 4Ps and consider four additional elements: **People, Physical evidence, Process** and **Packaging**.

Element	Explanation	Some considerations
Product	The goods/services offered	Brand, usefulness, features, guarantees, style, quality, functionality, warranty, durability, after-sale service, components
Price	The element of the marketing mix which is associated with generating revenue for the firms	Various pricing policies and strategies, e.g., competition and full costing policies
Promotion	Strategies which encourage the target market to purchase the firm's products/services	Advertising, sales promotion, referrals, public relations, networking, CSR activities, Internet, television
Place	Focus on channels which products and/or services meet the target audience	Wholesalers, retailers, agents, location, logistics, storage, market coverage, distribution
People	The people who are involved in the sale and provision of the goods/services	Level of training, communication skills, deportment, mannerisms, commitment, presence
Process	Procedures that ensure and support the efficiency of the firm's operation	Policies and procedures, systems, employee involvement
Physical evidence	The general appearance of external and internal environments in which the goods/services are offered to customers	Décor, packaging, location, cleanliness, ambience
Packaging	A number of variables which include, offering a combination of goods or services and placing goods in wrappers, boxes and bags. Packaging offers the advantage of differentiation	Type of material, colour, labels, design, combination, e.g., many tour operators around the world offer a combination of services as a package deal

Factors which determine the marketing mix adopted by a firm

√ The nature of goods or services to be marketed

√ The segment of the market to be targeted

√ The firm's marketing objectives

√ The marketing strategies of competitors

√ The cost associated with marketing the goods or services

The effectiveness of a selected marketing mix

A marketing mix is effective when the firm achieves the goals towards which the marketing mix was developed in implemented. For example, an effective marketing mix would result in:

√ Increased sales revenue

√ Successful penetration of a segment

√ Positive perception

√ Well established brand image.

You must be able to:

1. **Apply** the elements of the marketing mix to a given situation.

2. **Discuss** the effectiveness of a selected marketing mix in achieving marketing objectives. **(HL Only)**

3. **Construct** an appropriate marketing mix for a particular product or firm.

4. **Discuss** the effectiveness of a selected marketing mix in achieving strategic objectives.

The ethics of marketing

Ethical behaviour in marketing refers to how a firm applies a certain code of behaviour and principles to every aspect of its marketing activities.

Some ethical issues which should be considered by firms marketing their products/services nationally, internationally and across cultures are:

√ Considering the impact of their corporate actions on the environment

√ Implementing and respecting fair trading practices

√ Offering products/services which address the intended requirements

√ Offering safe and reliable products/services

√ Giving consumers value for money

√ Offering products and services in a safe environment

√ Sourcing ethical suppliers

√ Engaging in meaningful CSR initiatives

√ Adopting marketing practices which adhere to the law of the land

√ Respecting the culture and practices of current and potential customers.

NOTE: *Ethical approaches should be integrated throughout the marketing mix.*

You must be able to **discuss** the ethical issues of what is marketed and how it is marketed: nationally, internationally and across cultures.

© The IBO, 2007

Marketing audit

A marketing audit is the first step in the marketing planning process. The audit helps (a) analyse the internal and external marketing environments in which firm operates or seeks to operate and (b) identify elements which can significantly impact marketing efforts.

A marketing audit can be conducted by using a combination of tools, such as a SWOT analysis and PEST analysis.

The value of the marketing audit as a business tool

√ Aids the marketing planning process

√ Helps identify key competitors and their performance in the market

√ Helps identify new market segments towards which a firm can target products

√ Helps identify marketing strengths and weaknesses

You must be able to **explain** the value of a marketing audit as a business tool.

© The IBO, 2007

Porter's five forces
(HIGHER LEVEL FOCUS)

Michael Porter outlines five (5) forces which can significantly impact the competitive positions of individual businesses within their respective industries.

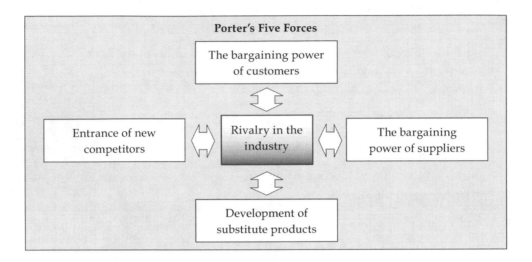

The bargaining power of **customers** influences the intensity of rivalry amongst competing firms, due to:

√ Changes in their perception of firms' products/services

√ Changes in their level of sensitivity to price changes over time

√ The fact that they have increasing access to substitute products

√ The fact that they can increase or decrease the amount of products/services they buy.

The extent to which **suppliers** influence the intensity of rivalry amongst competing firms depends on:

√ The number of suppliers available

√ Cost of raw materials/inputs

√ Threat of forward integration from suppliers

√ Availability of substitute raw materials/inputs.

The difficulty or ease with which **new competitors** enter the industry (hence, the intensity of rivalry amongst competing firms) is determined by the barriers which exist in the industry. Some examples of barriers to entry are:

√ Capital requirement   √ Economies of scale

√ Poor location   √ Lack of expertise

√ Stringent government policies   √ Customer loyalty.

The extent to which **substitute products** influence the intensity of rivalry amongst competing firms depends on factors such as:

√ The price of substitute products

√ The quality of substitute products

√ The switching cost to customers

√ The degree of customers' brand loyalty.

The **intensity of rivalry** amongst competing firms is influenced by factors such as:

√ The number of firms in the industry

√ The relative size and capability of firms in the industry

√ The decline in the demand for products/services offered by the industry

√ The strategies employed by each firm, e.g., differentiation strategies.

You must be able to **apply** Porter's five forces model to classify and analyse competitive pressures in the market place.

© The IBO, 2007

Marketing objectives

Marketing objectives are the goals a firm seeks to achieve through its marketing activities. Marketing objectives are determined in support of the firm's corporate objectives and are integral to its general business strategy. Therefore, like other business objectives, marketing objectives should be **SMART**.

Marketing objectives are developed in relation to issues such as:

√ Market share

√ Sales volume

√ Market segments

√ Product mix

√ Distribution

√ Technology to be employed.

√ Sales team

√ Sales revenue

The importance of marketing objectives

√ Set the direction and roadmap for the marketing team

√ Motivate management and staff towards specific marketing outcomes

√ Serve as the basis for developing and implementing marketing strategies

√ Enable monitoring and evaluating of marketing outcomes

√ Communicate the firm's marketing expectations for a specified period of time

Limitations of marketing objectives

The following factors can limit the extent to which a firm achieves its marketing objectives:

√ The budget allocated to marketing

√ Commitment of the marketing team and other employees to the firm's marketing goals

√ Economic factors, such as inflation, interest rates and economic growth

√ The nature of the firm

√ The firm's commitment to corporate social responsibility initiatives

√ Research-and-development capabilities of the firm.

You must be able to **examine** how appropriate marketing objectives are in achieving the goal of an organisation.

© The IBO, 2007

Market research

Market research relates to activities undertaken by a firm to find answers to questions pertaining to one or more marketing issues it faces. For example, customers perceptions about its products/services, customer-satisfaction levels, market segments, product suitability, market potential, trends and competitors.

The market-research process includes the following steps:

1. Identifying and defining the marketing problem
2. Collecting data from primary and/or secondary sources, using appropriate instruments and methodologies
3. Compiling and collating the data
4. Analysing the data
5. Communicating the results of the analysis to all relevant stakeholders.

The role of market research

√ Helps identify customer needs and wants

√ Enables formulating appropriate marketing strategies

√ Helps firms assess their position in the market

√ Provides a clear picture of competitors' performances

√ Drives innovation, research and development

Some limitations of market research

√ Management does not always have the financial and other logistical capabilities to implement the recommendations arising from market research.

√ The accuracy of data collected can contribute to the success or failure of research outcomes.

√ The research process is time consuming and expensive.

√ The results of the research are relative to a specified period of time.

√ Findings may not guarantee the best or the most appropriate marketing decisions.

You must be able to **analyse** the role of market research.   © The IBO, 2007

Primary and secondary research

Primary research: A process of gathering data that does not already exist. Primary research tools include questionnaires, face –to-face interviews, telephone interviews, online surveys, observations, focus groups and consumer panels.

Secondary research: A process of gathering information that already exists, to support current research into a particular issue facing the firm. Sources of secondary information include magazines, newspapers, business publications, government reports, trading-and-profit-and-loss accounts and balance sheets.

Primary research: Advantages

1. Original data is collected
2. Higher accuracy rate of information
3. Specific issues can be addressed

Secondary research: Advantages

1. Relatively inexpensive
2. Information readily available
3. May be easy to collate and evaluate information

Primary research: Disadvantages	Secondary research: Disadvantages
1. May be expensive	1. Possibility of biased information
2. Time consuming	2. Information may be outdated
3. May be limited by insufficient funding	3. Information may be too limited

You must be able to **evaluate** the different methods of market research. © The IBO, 2007

Sampling
(HIGHER LEVEL FOCUS)

Sampling is the process of selecting a representative group of individuals from within a population in order to gather data which will be used to make inferences about the population in general.

Methods of sampling

Quota sampling

The researcher works with a limited number of respondents who are to be selected based on certain characteristics or on subgroups to which they belong. There is a maximum or minimum limit on the quantity which can be selected from each group, e.g., selecting a sample of 25 males between the ages of 18 and 30.

Advantages

√ Relatively easy to organise and implement

√ Considered the most convenient method of sampling

√ Considered most reasonable in many instances

√ Considered ideal for obtaining a quick and reasonable response

Disadvantages

√ Possibility of bias by the interviewer when selecting the sample

√ Impossible to determine and evaluate sample errors (if any), due to the absence of randomness

√ The sample may not reflect the views of the whole population

√ Subjective, as it is based on the judgement of the interviewer

√ Call backs are difficult to organise

Random sampling

This is a method of sampling which gives each member of the defined population an equal chance of being selected.

Advantages

√ Facilitates the selection of a representative sample that reflects the highest probability

√ Ensures minimal difference between the sample and the population it represents

√ Eliminates bias on the part of the researcher

√ Helps draw inferences about the population, based on the behaviour of the sample

Disadvantages

√ Costly and time consuming

√ Dependent on accuracy of the the list of population from which the sample is to be drawn

√ Lack of skills of researcher using the technique (for example, using the table of random numbers)

Stratified sampling

Stratified sampling is a process of selecting a sample which equally represents all clearly defined subgroups (strata) as they exist in the population. For example, subgroups (strata) can represent age groups, geographic locations or occupations.

Advantages

√ Guarantees adequate representation of all subgroups in the population which is to be studied

√ Helps the researcher identify and work with subgroups that are relevant to the study

√ Enables easy administration, as each subgroup can be managed individually by the researcher

Disadvantages

√ Significant problems if the population and subgroups within the population are not clearly defined

√ May be expensive and complex

√ May be difficult to administer if researchers are not well trained in this methodology

Cluster sampling

This method of sampling divides the population into clusters, with members of each cluster exhibiting similar characteristics; subsequently, a random sample of the clusters is selected for the study.

Advantages	Disadvantages
√ Saves costs and time √ Convenient for large populations	√ Not as effective as random or stratified sampling √ Researchers do not always have sufficient control over subjects

Snowballing

Snowballing is a process whereby the researcher seeks one respondent's help in identifying other possible respondents from whom data can be obtained.

Advantages

√ Useful when the population under study is difficult to reach

√ Inexpensive when compared to other methods of sampling

Disadvantages

√ Sample may not be a true representation of the entire population

√ Reaching respondents can be time consuming and frustrating

Sampling errors

A sampling error refers to a condition where a sample differs significantly from the population, on some significant variable.

A major cause of sampling errors is sampling bias, which represents a situation where the researchers tend to favour and select samples that suit a pre-determined outcome.

Avoiding sampling errors

√ Selecting a relatively large representative sample

√ Being open-minded about the process. That is, the researcher should not have pre-conceived notions about the outcome.

You must be able to evaluate different methods of sampling   © The IEO, 2007

Market segmentation and consumer profile

Market segmentation refers to dividing the market into groups of customers or potential customers with similar needs and characteristics to which the business intends to responds.

METHODS OF SEGMENTATION	EXAMPLES
1. GEOGRAPHY	Continent, country, state, region, population density
2. DEMOGRAPHY	Age, gender, income levels, religion, social status, race, family size
3. PSYCHOLOGY	Values, opinions, interests
4. BEHAVIOUR	Frequency of use, benefit to be gained, brand loyalty, spending patterns

The usefulness of market segmentation

The following are some of the benefits of market segmentation:

√ Helps develop appropriate marketing strategies for specific targeted segments

√ Helps focus resources towards the most promising and lucrative segments of the market

√ Facilitates product and service differentiation which can lead to increased market share and profitability.

Consumer profile

For a business, consumer profile represents a collection of demographic, psychographic and geographic data about its customers. A consumer profile includes information such as:

√ Age   √ Sex   √ Income levels

√ Education levels   √ Purchasing patterns   √ Marital status

The usefulness of consumer profiles

The following are some of the benefits of consumer profile:

√ Helps identify and locate the most promising prospects

√ Facilitates market segmentation

√ Helps meet the specific needs of current and potential customers

√ Facilitates the development of new products

√ Enables developing new marketing strategies or revising existing ones.

You must be able to **analyse** the usefulness of market segmentation and consumer profiles.   © The IBO, 2007

Targeting

Targeting is the process of selecting a specific segment towards which significant marketing effort and resources will be committed with the hope of capturing or increasing the firm's share of the market.

The following are some factors which will be considered by a firm before it targets a specific segment of the market:

1. Availability of suitable resources, e.g., finance, human resources

2. Marketing objectives

3. Level of competition in the segment

4. Stability of the segment, that is, is it likely to change significantly in the short run?

5. Attractiveness and size of the segment

6. Profitability of the segment

7. Nature of the segment, e.g. location, age, spending patterns

8. Spending patterns within the segment.

NOTE: Effective market research is the key to successfully targeting a market segment.

You must be able to **identify** possible target market.   © The IBO, 2007

You must be able to **apply** appropriate marketing mix to the target market (s).   © The IBO, 2007

Product/service positioning

Positioning is about creating a positive perception in current and potential customer minds about the firm's products or services in relation to similar products or services offered by its competitors. Certain characteristics/features are used position products/services, for e.g., price, status factor, quality, benefits, usage)

The benefits of positioning

√ Competitive advantage.

√ Improvements in products and services e.g., features, packaging, usage.

√ Focus on innovation, research and development.

√ Favourable consumer perceptions, in cases where the product or service has been evaluated and repositioned.

√ New positions across different market segments can be considered.

√ Positive consumer perception and enhanced corporate image.

A product position map

Product position map is a visual representation of a company's product or service position in the market as compared with its competitors.

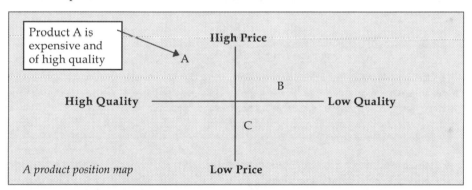

A product position map

Strategies for changing customer perceptions
(HIGHER LEVEL FOCUS)

√ Using the most effective media to provide timely, accurate, relevant information about products/services.

√ Repositioning the product/service.

√ Engaging in or improving Corporate Social Responsibility (CSR) initiatives.

√ Improving quality and adopting effective pricing strategies.

Corporate image

Corporate image refers to how a firm is perceived by members of the public, collectively and individually.

The value of corporate image

An organisation with a positive corporate image benefits in the following ways:

- √ Brand-loyalty benefits
- √ Committed and reliable suppliers
- √ Committed and motivated employees
- √ Increased customer base and profitability
- √ Government support if and when needed
- √ Easy to position the firm's products or services.

NOTE: One of the major strategies adopted by business organisations to improve their corporate image is sustained Corporate Social Responsibility initiatives.

Unique Selling Point/Proposition (USP)

A unique selling point/proposition refers to features of the organisation, its products/services which distinguish it from its competitors. A firm's USP is established through the development and implementation of an appropriate marketing mix.

Organisations can differentiate themselves from competitors by developing and implementing the following strategies:

√ **Cost-leadership strategies**, e.g., low cost of production, low-priced suppliers

√ **Differentiation strategies**, e.g., differentiation on pricing, brand name, technology, service, corporate image

√ **Focus strategies**, e.g., focusing resources towards capturing specific segment of the market.

You must be able to **discuss** how organisations can differentiate themselves and their products from competitors.

Development of marketing strategies and tactics

Marketing strategies: These are the **long-term** action plans a firm develops and implements towards achieving its marketing objectives. For example, adopting a penetration pricing strategy to enter a new market.

Marketing tactics: These are the **short-term** marketing activities which are developed and implemented to support the marketing strategies of a firm. For example, the firm offers a 10% discount on a product during the Christmas season.

The marketing strategies and tactics developed and implemented by a firm are largely dependent on:

√ Strength of competitors in the industry

√ Availability of similar or substitute products

√ Nature of the product or service to be marketed

√ Level of current and potential demand for the product or service

√ Economic conditions, e.g., level of inflation, economic growth or decline

√ The nature of the segment (s) of the market to be targeted, e.g., spending patterns and life styles.

√ Marketing objectives

√ Availability of funding

√ Nature and size of the firm

NOTE: A firm's marketing strategies and tactics are communicated through its marketing plan. From the plan the strategies and tactics are then developed and implemented.

Some tools which are used to aid the design and evaluation of marketing strategies and tactics are:

Tool	Use
1. Porter's generic strategies	Development of competitive strategies
2. Porter's five forces model	Competitor analysis
3. Ansoff matrix	Development of market growth strategies
4. Boston matrix (BCG matrix)	Analysis of product portfolio.

You must be able to **design** or **evaluate** marketing strategies for a given situation. Apply appropriate marketing mix to the strategy.

Sales forecasting and trends
(HIGHER LEVEL FOCUS)

Sales forecasting: This is an estimate of what sales will be in some future time. Sales forecasting takes into account the historical data (the past sales performance) to estimate future sales levels.

Sales trends: These refer to sales patterns over a period of time.

The benefits of sales forecasting

√ Identifies sales trends.

√ Reduces operational costs.

√ Enhances production planning.

√ Enhances sales revenue and profit.

√ Enhances a firm's chances of acquiring funding.

√ Leads to efficiency, e.g., stock control and capacity.

Some quantitative techniques for sales forecasting

1. **The time-series analysis:** This technique uses historical sales data, which is collected on a consistent basis, e.g., every month, to forecast the value of sales for a particular period in the future. The results of a time-series analysis indicates the following.

   a) *Trends:* A consistent pattern (increase or decrease) of sales over a long period of time.

   b) *Seasonal variations:* Increases or decreases in demand which can be correlated with certain times during the year, e.g., increases in the demand for kites during the Easter season in the Caribbean.

   c) *Cyclical variation:* Increase or decrease in demand which can be correlated to periods in the business cycle.

   d) *Random variation:* Short-term increases or decreases in sales due to favourable or unfavourable occurrences, such as a decrease in price or a sudden strike.

2. **Moving averages:** The average of a set of numbers, over a period of time, which is constantly updated by **dropping the oldest data, adding the newest data** and then **recalculating the average**.

The moving average clearly reflects sales trends, by removing any fluctuations (smoothing) in the data.

Calculation of moving average

A three (3) points moving average based on the yearly sales of a furniture company

Year	Sales
2001	12,000
2002	10,000
2003	15,000
2004	32,000
2005	18,000
2006	44,000

12,000 + 10,000 + 15,000/3 = **12, 333.3**

Drop the oldest data $ 12,000 and recalculate the average:

10,000 + 15,000 + 32,000/3 = **19,000**

Drop the oldest data $ 10,000 and recalculate the average:

15,000 + 32,000 + 18,000/3 = **21,667**

Drop the oldest data $ 15,000 and recalculate the average:

32,000 + 18,000 + 44,000/3 = **31,333**

Interpretation: The moving average, in this case, indicates the trend in sale over a 6-year period.

Extrapolation

Uses historical sales data to calculate and extend sales trends into the future.

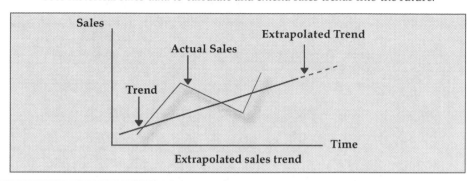

Extrapolated sales trend

The significance of sales trends and forecasts in marketing and resource planning

√ Help businesses to deal effectively with competition

√ Aid planning in areas, such as recruitment, budgetary allocations, production and marketing

√ Encourage the development and implementation of innovative business strategies

√ Facilitate managing cash flow

√ Help target new market segments

You must be able to **analyse** trends and forecasts from given data, and evaluate the significance for marketing and resources planning.

4.3: PRODUCT

A product is a good or service offered for sale by businesses to current and potential customers.

Classification of products

Classification	Explanation	Examples
Product line	A group of related products	Coca-Cola: Diet Coke, Coca-Cola Zero, Coca-Cola BlaK
Product mix	A combination of different products offered for sale by a company	Samsung: Cell phones, cameras, televisions, computers, refrigerators, washing machines
Product range	The different variety of products sold by the firm	General Electric: different lines and mixes of electrical equipment, accessories and tools

You must be able to **classify** products by line, range and mix.

New-product design and development

New product design

This includes all the processes associated with designing and developing new products. Like any production process, the design and development of new products is geared towards **adding value** to the **product or service** with the aim of retaining current customers and attracting new customers.

Benefits of new product design and development

Some of the benefits of designing and developing a new product are:

√ Enhanced brand image and reputation

√ Investment in new technologies

√ Wider product portfolio for multi- product firms

√ Increase in profits

√ Economies of scale and scope

√ Significant tax benefits from the costs associated with product design and development efforts.

Innovation and Research and Development (R&D)

Innovation and research and development are the catalysts which drive any effort towards the design and development of new products. In this era of rapid technological changes, innovation and research and development can bring the following benefits to a firm:

√ Improve productivity

√ Reduced cost of production

√ Significant improvements to products and services

√ Availability of a wider variety of goods and services

√ Considerable competitive advantage in the industry.

Factors affecting Research and Development (R&D)

√ Lack of funding

√ Management's lack of support for innovative ideas and R&D efforts

√ Declining economic trends significantly reduce R&D budgets

√ The role of R&D in achieving corporate objectives

√ Success or failure of past R&D initiatives

You must be able to:

1. **Describe** the importance of innovation in an era of rapid technological change.

2. **Discuss** the problems of financing research and development.

Product Life Cycle

The product life cycle is a marketing model which represents the various stages a product passes through from its development and introduction into the market to its decline and withdrawal from the market.

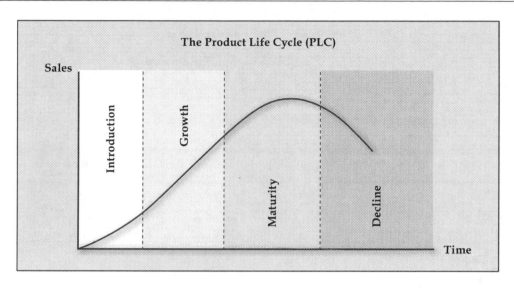

Activities at various stages of the Product Life Cycle (PLC)

Activities	Introduction	Growth	Maturity	Decline
Nature of consumers	Early adopters	Mainstream	Late adopters	Laggards
Market size	Small	Growing	Large	Contracting
Marketing Focus	Awareness	Differentiation	Brand loyalty	Divesting
Competition	Low	Moderate	Intense	Reduced
Sales revenue	Low	Moderate	High	Reduced
Investment	High	High	Moderate	Low
Profit	None -low	Moderate	High	Reduced
Cash flow	Low	Moderate	High	Decline

The relationship between product life cycle and marketing mix

Marketing Mix	Introduction	Growth	Maturity	Decline
Product	One	Product development	Full product line	New product development
Price	Market based	Market based	Competition based	Promotional pricing
Promotion	Awareness	Differentiation	Defensive	Maintain sales revenue/Profit
Place	Limited outlets	Many outlets	Maximum outlets	Reduced number of outlets

Extension strategies: Keeping the product alive

Extension strategies are action plans which are designed and implemented with the aim of preventing a product or service from declining. Effective extension strategies are those which are given considerable research and development support by management.

Examples of extension strategies

√ Finding new market segments for the product or service

√ Finding new uses for the product or service

√ Adding new features, colour, and ingredients to the product

√ Selling the product under a new label

The product life cycle: relationship with investment, profit and cash flow

INTRODUCTION

Investment: Considerable investment in advertising and promotion.

Profit: Profit may be realised but may not be very high.

Cash flow: Cash flow may be positive, due to increase in cash sales.

MATURITY

Investment: Moderate investment towards the development and implementation of extension strategies.

Profit: Profit increases at a slow rate.

Cash flow: Cash flow remains positive.

GROWTH

Investment: Considerable investment in activities aimed at differentiation.

Profit: Considerable increase in profit. However, profitability depends on the effectiveness of the marketing strategies employed by the firm.

Cash flow: Cash flow is positive.

DECLINE

Investment: Spending is very low or nil.

Profit: Declines at this phase. Strategies must be employed to keep profit stable.

Cash flow: Cash flow declines.

You must be able to:

1. **Analyse** the relationship between the product life cycle and the marketing mix and determine appropriate extension strategies.

2. **Analyse** the relationship between the product life cycle, investment, profit and cash flow.

© The IBO, 2007

Product portfolio analysis

Boston Consulting Group Matrix (BCG matrix)

The Boston Consulting Group (BCG) Matrix is a measuring grid and a useful tool for analysing, planning and managing a company's range of products (product portfolio) or business units. The matrix focuses on two variables - **market growth** and **market share**.

The Boston Consulting Group (BCG) Matrix

	High Market Share	**Low** Market Share
High Market Growth	**STAR** High market growth High market share Strong cash flow and profits High investment	**PROBLEM CHILD** High market growth Low market share Relatively new product Low cash flow
Low Market Growth	**CASH COW** High market share Low market growth Stable income generated Income often used to support problem child	**DOG** Low market share Low market growth Cash flow is virtually negative

Advantages of BCG matrix

√ Facilitates marketing decisions

√ Helps marketing managers evaluate a firm's product range

√ Easy to understand and use

Disadvantages of BCG matrix

√ Assumes that high profits are associated with high market shares; this assumption may not be applicable to all types of businesses.

√ Market growth and market share are not the only factors to be used to evaluate the relative success of a group of products or services.

√ Assumes that businesses with a low market share are not profitable; this assumption may not be applicable to all businesses.

You must be able to **apply** the BCG matrix to a given situation.   © The IBO, 2007

Using the Boston Consulting Group Matrix to develop future strategic direction
(HIGHER LEVEL FOCUS)

	STAR	PROBLEM CHILD
High	**Possible strategies**	**Possible strategies**
	Aggressive advertising and promotion	Invest more money if the product shows good potential
	Further research and development	
	Expand output and sales	Drop the product from the portfolio
	CASH COW	**DOG**
	Possible strategies	**Possible strategies**
	Use the cash generated here to support other products which show good potential	Retain the product in the portfolio to achieve brand recognition
		Invest if there is a possibility of gaining market share
Low	Advertise and promote to maintain market position	Liquidate – drop the product completely

Market Growth ↑

High ————— Market Share ————→ **Low**

You must be able to use the BCG matrix to help in developing future strategic direction. © The IBO, 2007

Branding

According to the American Marketing Association (AMA), a brand is a name, term, sign, symbol or design, or a combination of them, intended to identify the goods and services of one seller or group of sellers and to differentiate them from those of other sellers.

Brand awareness

This is the extent to which current and potential customers know of the existence and availability of a firm's products/services.

Strategies for promoting brand awareness

Companies can adopt a number of strategies to promote brand awareness. Outstanding brands (for example, Nike and Sony) resonate with current and potential customers because the companies selling the brands are engaged in activities such as aggressive advertising, promotion and involvement in a number of CSR initiatives. Brand awareness provides a number of advantages:

√ Increases in sales, profit, market share √ Loyal customer base √ Market leadership.

Brand development

Brand development is the process of clearly defining, reviewing and establishing a brand to enhance its position amongst competing brands.

Brand development strategies

1. A clear definition or redefinition of the brand
2. Appropriate packaging, pricing, promotion
3. Appropriate positioning
4. Research and development
5. Effective communication of the brand's value
6. Analysis of similar brands in the market

The following are some of the advantages of brand development:

√ Enhances brand image

√ Enhances the customer perception of the product/service

√ Helps offer better products/services to current and future customers.

√ Increases sales and profit

√ Provides a competitive edge

Brand loyalty

A key component of a firm's competitive advantage: brand loyalty is the commitment of customers to a firm's product or product line. For example, customers who are committed to the Nike brand may not purchase a Reebok product.

Strategies for developing and sustaining brand loyalty

1. Employing appropriate pricing, promotion and advertising strategies
2. Maintaining or improving customer perception by offering quality products/services
3. Constantly developing new or related products/services
4. Engaging in CSR initiatives

The advantages a firm gains from customer loyalty to its brand are numerous. For example:

√ Increases awareness about the firm's products or services

√ Improves the firm's competitive position

√ Innovation and product development

√ Increases sales revenue and profit.

The importance and role of branding

√ Creates customer loyalty

√ Increases sales revenue and profits

√ Establishes a strong corporate identity

√ Differentiates the firm's products or services from those of its competitors

√ Improves a firm's competitive advantage and brand equity amongst competing brands

You must be able to **discuss** the importance and role of branding. © The IBO, 2007

Types of branding
(HIGHER LEVEL FOCUS)

Family branding

This refers to selling a range of products or services under the same brand name. For example, Samsung produces and sells a range of products and services under the Samsung brand.

Advantages

√ Offers significant economies of scope and reduction in costs. A common set of advertisements and campaigns can be used to promote several products under the same brand name.

√ Facilitates introducing new products/services in the market. Any new product sold under the existing brand name may attract the attention of current and future customers who are familiar with the brand name.

Disadvantages

√ If the quality of one product is compromised, customers may form negative perceptions about other products in the portfolio, resulting in a significant drop in sales across the brand.

Product branding

Products within a product portfolio are promoted and sold under exclusive brand names. When new products are introduced into the portfolio, they are branded differently from existing products. For example, Yum! Brands Inc is a restaurant which promotes and sells fast foods of major restaurant brands, such as KFC, Pizza Hut, Long John Silver and Taco Bell.

Advantages

√ Each brand is promoted on its own merit, without being influenced by other brands within the portfolio.

√ Each product in the portfolio is considered unique, serving the business well in terms of the position it occupies amongst competing products.

√ Financial gain from brand equity is a major benefit to be derived from product branding.

Disadvantages

√ Increased marketing cost, due to the need to promote and advertise each product separately. Each product demands a separate advertising and promotion budget.

√ New products introduced into the portfolio cannot leverage the benefits (for example, positive sales) associated with other products in the portfolio.

Company (Corporate) branding

In this branding approach, the brand name of the product or service is the same as that of the company. For example, Coca Cola beverages are branded with the name of the company.

Advantages

√ The cost and other activities involved in promoting and selling one product can be applied to all other products of the company – economies of scope.

(Contd...)

√ Any new product introduced into the product mix may attract the attention of current and future customers who are familiar with the company and its products.

√ Brand loyalty is developed from customer's familiarity with the company and its products or services.

√ The firm's corporate image is boosted.

Disadvantages

√ Customers perceive all products under the corporate brand as essentially sharing the same characteristics.

√ Customers assume that all products in a portfolio are of the same quality. Consequently, a poor quality product can significantly affect the sales of all other products in the portfolio.

Own (Private) label branding

In this branding approach, products and/or services are sold under the name of the firm. Typically, big supermarket chains, such as Tesco and Sainsbury, sell products labelled with their brand names, e.g., Sainsbury butter or oil.

Advantages

√ Businesses (such as Tesco and Sainsbury) have the freedom and flexibility with regard to costing, pricing, quality and quantity of their products.

√ These supermarkets know how best to develop and promote their brands.

√ There is no competition since other businesses cannot carry the brand.

√ Each brand is exclusive to specific supermarket chains.

Disadvantages

√ A solid customer base must be established to support the brand.

√ Significant amount of resources are required to promote a private brand.

√ Start-up businesses require significant time to establish their brands amongst other competing brands.

Manufacturer's brand

In this branding approach, goods are branded and sold under the manufacturer's name.

Advantage: Wider product recognition and customer base as wholesalers and retailers distribute the products.

Disadvantage: Considerable costs and other resources to establish the brand.

You must be able to:

1. **Distinguish** between different types of branding.

2. **Analyse** the role of branding in a global market place.

4.4: PRICE

Price is the amount of money which must be paid by customers for goods or services.

The importance of pricing

The pricing of goods and services is important for a number of reasons:

√ Differentiating the firm's products or services from those of its competitors

√ Increasing sales and revenue

√ Ensuring the firm's profitability

√ Use as a survival strategy.

Pricing strategies

A pricing strategy refers to any decision taken by a firm to ensure the most realistic and competitive prices for the goods and services it offers for sale. When determining the most appropriate pricing strategy, a firm considers factors such as:

√ Segment of the target market

√ Availability of similar or substitute products

√ Current and future consumer expectations

√ The nature and characteristics of the product or service

√ Legal factors, such as the existence of price regulation legislation

√ Ease with which new firms can enter or exit the market within the short run.

√ Pricing strategies of competitors

√ Bargaining power of key suppliers

Cost based pricing policy

Adopting a cost-based pricing policy means that a firm sets the price of its products based on the cost of producing each unit. That is, a predetermined percentage mark-up is added to the cost of producing each unit of output.

Cost based pricing strategies

1. Cost - Plus strategy
2. Marginal-cost pricing strategy
3. Absorption pricing strategy
4. Full-cost pricing strategy

Cost plus pricing strategy

The total cost (Fixed Cost + Variable Costs) of each unit of output is determined, and then a fixed increment or percentage of this cost is added to determine the selling price.

Example: For Caribbean Furniture Traders Ltd., the cost of manufacturing a chair is $25.00. The management, after considering all financial and non-financial factors, has decided that a 75% mark-up would be appropriate. Determine the price which should be charged per chair.

Answer: In this case, the selling price would be $ 43.75.

(Contd...)

Advantages

√ Provides a simple way of calculating the selling price of goods or services

√ Easy to understand and implement

√ Considers all the costs while determining the selling price

√ Ensures that some level of profit is realised

Disadvantages

√ If the per-unit production cost is not accurately calculated, the selling price could result in price per unit below that which is enough to recover cost

√ Does not consider the current and future demand for goods and services

---

Marginal cost or Contribution pricing strategy
(HIGHER LEVEL FOCUS)

A marginal cost is a cost associated with the production of an extra unit of good or service.

Marginal-cost pricing strategy: The selling price of a unit of good is based on the variable cost associated with the increase in production by an extra unit and the contribution which is needed to cover fixed cost and profit.

Example: Each unit of chair produced by Caribbean Furniture Traders Ltd. has a variable cost of $15.00. If the company intends to make a contribution of $35.00 towards fixed cost and profit, each chair must be sold at $50.00 each.

If the company incurs a fixed cost of $60,000 per year and if it produces and sells 5000 units of chairs, the total contribution amounts to $175,000 ($35.00 x 5000 units). Consequently, the company makes a profit of ($175,000 - $60,000) = $115,000.

Marginal cost or Contribution pricing strategy

Advantages

√ All variable costs are ascertained and covered in the established price.

√ There is flexibility in pricing of individual products and services.

√ The average price reflects only the additional variable costs.

Marginal cost or Contribution pricing strategy

Disadvantages

√ Flexible pricing is not necessarily the most effective pricing strategy, as set prices may not cover the fixed cost adequately.

√ Contribution pricing is a short-term pricing strategy.

Full cost pricing strategy
(HIGHER LEVEL FOCUS)

Full cost pricing is a strategy which allocates overheads (indirect cost) to each unit of production, based on the random allocation of one criterion. Once the indirect cost is apportioned and allocated to each unit of output, it is then added to a predetermined mark up to arrive at the selling price.

Example: A firm produces two products, A and B. The direct cost of producing one unit of product A is $10.00 and one unit of B is $ 15.00. The total overhead (indirect) cost is $3000, which is equally allocated to products A and B. The quarterly output is 700 units of A and 1000 units of B.

Determine the selling price per unit of A and B given that the predetermined mark ups are set at 20% per unit of product A and 40% per unit of product B.

Answer

Cost	Product A	Product B
Total direct cost	$ 7,000	$ 15,000
Allocation of indirect cost (basis 50%)	$ 1,500	$ 1,500
Total cost	$ 8,500	$ 16,500
Cost per unit	**$ 12.14**	**$ 16.50**
% Mark-up	$ 2.43	$ 6.60
Selling price per unit	**$ 14.57**	**$ 23.10**

Advantages

√ Once the criterion for allocating indirect cost is decided, determining the selling price is easy.

√ Full-cost pricing allows for the appropriate allocation and management of cost to respective cost centres, e.g., products.

√ Price per unit of output reflects the total cost associated with producing that unit of output.

√ Management has full knowledge of all costs when making the pricing decision.

Disadvantages

√ Does not guarantee the most appropriate pricing

√ Poses the danger of setting prices based on inaccurate allocation of costs

√ Unsuitable for short-term pricing decisions

√ Ignores qualitative factors such as the state of competition and changes in consumer demand

Absorption cost pricing strategy
(HIGHER LEVEL FOCUS)

The absorption cost pricing strategy is based on the total cost per unit of output by calculating and allocating fixed manufacturing overhead to each unit of output. Unlike the full cost pricing method, this strategy does not encourage an arbitrary allocation of overheads.

Moreover, overheads are allocated using some rational basis of apportionment. For example, if a business manufactures multiple products and the products pass through a number of departments during the manufacturing process, the overhead incurred by each department is calculated and allocated to each product.

Some bases of apportionment may include floor area of each department, number of employees in each department and power consumption of each department.

Example: A firm produces two products, A and B. The direct cost of producing one unit of product A is $10.00 and the direct cost of producing one unit of B is $15.00. The breakup of the total overhead (indirect) cost of $5000 is as follows:

Cost	Cost
Wages and salaries	$ 2000
Electricity cost	$ 700
Advertising & promotion cost	$ 1000
Factory rent	$ 800
Water rates	$ 500

In addition to the overhead costs associated with the production of A and B, the following information must be considered:

1. The factory spans 2000 square meters, which is shared on a 50% basis for each product

2. Product A uses 6000 kWh of electricity while product B uses 10,000 kWh

3. Water rates incurred are allocated on a 50% basis

4. The factory employs 25 workers; while 10 are assigned to the production of A, 15 are assigned to the production of B

5. Advertising and promotion costs are allocated as 40% to product A and 60% to product B

6. The output per quarter is 1000 units of A and 1500 units of B.

Using this information, determine the selling price per unit of these products at a predetermined mark up of 30% for per unit of product A and 40% per unit of product B.

Answer

Overheads	Costs	Basis of apportionment	Product A	Product B
Wages and salaries	$ 2000	Number of employees	$ 800	$ 1,200
Electricity cost	$ 700	kWh used	$ 262.50	$ 437.50
Advertising/promotion	$ 1000	Output produced and sold per quarter	$ 400	$ 600
Factory rent	$ 800	Factory space	$ 400	$ 400
Water rates	$ 500	Factory space	$ 250	$ 250
Total overhead costs	$ 5,000		$ 2,112.50	$ 2,887.50
Total direct cost			$10,000	$ 22,500
Total cost			**$ 12,112.50**	**$ 25,387.50**
Cost per unit			$ 12.11	$ 16.92
% Mark-up			$ 3.63	$ 6.76
Selling price			**$ 15.74**	**$ 23.68**

Absorption cost pricing strategy

Advantages

√ Considers all production costs to determine the selling price per unit of output

√ The cost associated with each cost centre and unit of output can be managed more effectively.

Disadvantages

√ No definite rules regarding how overheads should be apportioned and allocated.

√ Pricing is based solely on the total cost and does not consider other factors which could influence pricing decisions (for example, the state of competition in the market).

Competition-based pricing policy

Competition-based pricing policies are set in relation to competitors. In this approach, a firm uses the prices which are offered by its competitors as the basis for setting the prices of its own products or services.

Competition-based pricing strategies

1. Price-leadership strategy

2. Predatory pricing strategy

3. Going-rate pricing strategy

Price leadership strategy

Firms that dominate the market are well poised to adopt a price-leadership strategy. These firms set the price of their products and services at very competitive rates, and their competitors are often obliged to respond by setting similar prices for their goods or services.

Advantage

√ The firm's position is maintained or further strengthened amongst its competitors.

Disadvantage

√ Firms which are considered as price leaders are always under intense scrutiny by the government and the public for any incidence of unfair pricing practices.

Predatory pricing strategy
(HIGHER LEVEL FOCUS)

In this strategy, a firm reduces the prices of its goods and services to such a level that its competitors find it difficult to continue competing at that price.

Predatory pricing is also known as destroyer pricing, and businesses employ this strategy with the intent of eliminating their competitors from the market.

Advantages

√ Increases the market share

√ Deters new firms from entering the market – barrier to entry

Disadvantages

√ Anti-competitive

√ Low or no profit margin

Going rate pricing strategy
(HIGHER LEVEL FOCUS)

This strategy allows a firm to price its products based on the prices (going rate) set by similar firms within the industry.

Advantage

√ Opportunity to take advantage of a price structure that has been tested and established

Disadvantages

√ The firm cannot compete on price; consequently, customers make the buying decision based on their perceptions of the products or services offered by the firm

√ Considerable time and resources involved in assessing the reliability of the prices charged by similar firms

√ Does not consider the costs involved in creating the goods or services

Market based pricing policy

Market-based pricing policies are based on the firm's assessment and analysis of the market.

1. Penetration pricing strategy
2. Skimming pricing strategy
3. Price discrimination
4. Loss leader pricing strategy
5. Psychological pricing strategy
6. Promotional pricing strategy

Penetration pricing

In this approach, the product is priced low with the intention that it will gain a considerable share of the market. Usually, this strategy is adopted to launch a new product/service.

Advantages

√ Enables new products to gain a significant market share

√ Increases customer base.

Disadvantages

√ Considered anti-competitive

√ Profits are sacrificed at the expense of gaining initial market share

√ The low price does not guarantee that the product or service penetrates the market

Skimming pricing strategy

Initially, a high price is set for the product/service; as the product/service is established in the market or as the market gets saturated, the price is gradually reduced.

Skimming is a short-term pricing strategy that is adopted when a firm launches a new product/service.

Advantages

√ The advantage of early demand increases sales revenue and profit, in the short run

√ Quick recovery of investment costs

√ New firms may be deterred from entering the market, in the short run

Disadvantages

√ A short-term pricing strategy

√ A high price may force current and potential customers to buy alternative products or services

Price discrimination
(HIGHER LEVEL FOCUS)

Price discrimination is a strategy of selling the same products or services at different prices to different segments of the market.

Advantages

√ Scope for increase in sales and revenue

√ Some segments benefit from the lower prices

Disadvantages

√ Successful only if the firm has a considerable market share, and no alternative products or services are available to customers.

√ Considerable time and resources involved in planning and implementing price discrimination strategies for each segment of the market.

Loss leader pricing strategy
(HIGHER LEVEL FOCUS)

Loss leader pricing is a strategy whereby the firm prices its products or services below the standard price at which it would realise some level of profit. This is short-run pricing strategy aimed at attracting customers.

Advantage

√ Increases customers and sales volume

Disadvantages

√ The cost associated with the goods or services is not considered.

√ If the product's scope is limited, the strategy cannot be continued for a long time.

√ The business loses money on each sale.

Psychological pricing strategy
(HIGHER LEVEL FOCUS)

Psychological pricing strategies appeal to consumer emotions rather than their rational thinking. For example, when a firm prices its products at $ 1.99 per unit, customers feel the product is relatively cheap as they are not paying $ 2.00.

Advantages

√ Attracts customers

√ Increases sales volume

Disadvantage

√ May not be appropriate for all categories of goods and services

Promotional pricing strategy
(HIGHER LEVEL FOCUS)

Promotional pricing method is often used to increase sales volume. This strategy may also be used by firms when they are clearing house, that is, they are seeking to sell off excess or slow-moving stocks.

Advantages

√ Customers take advantage of low prices

√ Effective in sell off of excess or slow moving goods

Disadvantage

√ Short-term pricing strategy

You must be able to:

1. **Analyse** the appropriateness of each pricing strategy.

2. **Analyse** the appropriateness of each pricing policy (HL ONLY).

Demand and supply
(HIGHER LEVEL FOCUS)

Price determination: This is the interaction of the forces of **demand** and **supply** which determine the market price level.

Demand: The amount of goods and services people are willing and able to purchase at a given price and time.

Supply: The amounts of goods or services producers are willing to make available at a given price and time.

Determinants of demand

The following are some factors which determine the willingness of consumers to demand a good or service:

Price

As the price of a product or service decreases, the demand increases. On the other hand, as the price increases, the demand falls.

Non-priced factors/Conditions of demand

A **condition of demand** is any factor, other than the price, that affects the demand for a good or service. Some conditions of demand are:

1. Income of consumers	2. Number of customers
3. Complements	4. Market trends: consumer tastes, perception, fashion
5. Consumer expectations	6. Substitutes.

Change in condition of demand	Impact on businesses
Change in consumers' income	A fall in consumers' income diminishes their purchasing power, resulting in reduced sales volume, revenue and profits for the firm. A rise in consumers' income increases the demand for goods and services, increasing the firm's revenue and short-term profits.
Change in the number of customers	When a firm loses customers, it is likely to experience a decrease in demand for its goods or services. Consequently, the firm's profit and revenue decreases. An increase in customer base bolsters the demand, which has a positive impact on the firm's revenue and profit.
The price of related goods: Complements and Substitutes	If the price of a good falls, the demand for related goods may also fall. Example: If the price of bananas falls, consumers buy more bananas even if they are used to buying some other fruit. Consequently, the vendors in other fruit markets may experience a drop in sales volume, revenue and profits. A similar situation arises from an increase or decrease in the price of complementary goods and services.
Market trends: Changes in consumer tastes, perception, fashion	Changing market trends drive the demand for a firm's goods or services. Changing fashion, perceptions and taste reflect the overall demand in the market, resulting in an adverse or a favourable impact on revenue and profits.
Consumer expectations	Consumer expectations about the future affect the demand for certain goods and services, for example, the anticipation of a drought may increase the demand for certain crops.

A change in any **condition of demand** results in an **increase** or **decrease** in demand

An increase in demand: Benefits to businesses

√ Higher revenues and profits

√ Increased wages and benefits for employees

√ More financial resources for research and development

√ Improvements in market research

√ Innovative products and services

√ New technology

Sustained increase in demand: Limitations and associated costs

√ Increased costs associated with accommodating increases in demand

√ Labour unions bargaining for higher wages and benefits for the employees

√ Focus on meeting consumer demand while neglecting the needs of employees who may be under pressure and stressed out due to increased workload

√ Machinery and other systems working at full capacity may lead to frequent breakdowns due to insufficient time for maintenance and repairs.

Decrease in demand: Opportunities for changes in strategies

A drop in demand encourages a firm to explore the following possibilities.

√ Revisit their marketing strategies, e.g., lower prices, add new features, use new or additional distribution channels, promote to new segments.

√ Drop the product completely – liquidate.

√ Diversify, e.g., offer other products or services.

√ Move into completely new businesses.

NOTE: The impact of changes in the **conditions of demand** depends on the nature of the change (temporary or permanent).

Decrease in demand: Impact on businesses

√ Lower sales levels

√ Decrease in revenue and profits

√ Limited funding for expansion, research and development

√ Bankruptcy, in some cases

Determinants of supply

The supply of goods/services is determined by the following factors:

Price

More products/services are supplied at a higher price.

Non-priced factors/Conditions of supply

A **condition of supply** is any factor that affects the supply of a good or service. Some conditions of supply are listed below:

1. Cost of raw materials
2. State of technology employed
3. Level of subsidies offered by the government
4. Taxes
5. Price of other goods
6. Number of suppliers.

A change in any condition of supply results in an increase or decrease in supply.

For example, a reduction in tax on the production of certain products may encourage businesses to produce and supply more of those products, due to lower production cost. An increase in tax is likely to have the opposite effect.

An increase in supply: Impact on businesses

√ Provides the opportunity for increasing supply at prices that ensure higher revenues and profits, in the short-run

√ Encourages adopting better technology

√ Encourages innovation

√ Availability of the product in surplus results in a drop in prices

A decrease in supply: Impact on businesses

√ Some firms will be forced out of the market as they may not be able to cope with, for example, higher cost of raw materials or higher taxes.

√ When a shortage is created, firms which can absorb the negative changes in any condition of demand are likely to benefit from supplying less at higher prices.

The relationship between supply and demand

After conducting its marketing research, a jewellery company decides to produce 100 diamond rings that would be priced at $2000 each for the Christmas season. If 500 rings are demanded, the company is likely to raise the price, in response to the increase in demand. In this scenario the company would obviously want to address the increased demand by increasing its production and supply of the rings.

On the other hand, suppose the company failed to conduct a thorough market research and produces 500 diamond rings. If the quantity demanded is only 100, the company would be forced to lower the price to attract customers.

In theory, the amount of goods/services demanded may equal the amount of goods/services that the producers are willing to and are able to supply. This relationship between demand and supply is referred to as equilibrium.

You must be able to **evaluate** the impact of changes in the condition of supply and demand.   © The IBO, 2007

Remember, diagrams are not required here.

Elasticity
(HIGHER LEVEL FOCUS)

Elasticity is a measure of response. That is, it is a measure of how the change in one factor creates the change in another factor.

Price elasticity of demand: Measures the response of **quantity demanded** to a **difference in price.**

$$\text{PED} = \frac{\text{\% Change in Quantity demanded}}{\text{\% Change in Price}}$$

Question

A horse racing company experienced an increase in the demand for tickets from 1,000 to 1,500 in one season after management decided to reduce the price from $200.00 to $150.00 per ticket. Calculate the price elasticity of demand and interpret your results.

1. Calculate the percentage (%) change in Quantity Demanded (Δ in Qd/Qd)

Old **Qd**	New **Qd**	(New **Qd** – Old **Qd**) ÷ Old **Qd**
1000	1500	(1500-1000)÷1000 = 500/1000 =0.5

2. Calculate the percentage (%) change in Price ($\Delta P/P$)

Old ($) **P**	New ($) **P**	(New **P** – Old **P**) ÷ Old **P**
200	150	(150-200)÷200 = -50/200 = -0.25

3. Using the formula PED = % Change in Quantity Demanded / % Change in Price = 0.5/0.25 = 2

NOTE: While calculating price elasticity, always ignore the negative signs.

Interpretation of the results

When the percentage change in quantity demanded is greater than the percentage change in price, demand is said to be **elastic**.

In this case, the demand for tickets is said to be elastic (PED is more than 1). This means that consumers have responded to the decrease in price by demanding more of the commodity. Management of this company is therefore likely to see an increase in sales revenue, unless it decides to keep the price at $200 per ticket or increase it further.

PED values and what they mean for businesses

PED value	Elasticity	Meaning	Likely response of businesses	Effects
Zero to one	Inelastic	% change in Q is less than % change in P	A business which faces an inelastic demand for its products can increase the price.	No significant reduction in quantity demanded. Increased revenue.
One	Unitary	% change in Q is equal to % change in P	Firms are likely to hold price constant.	No effect on Qd. No effect on Price. No effect on sales revenue.
One to infinity	Elastic	% change in Q is greater than % change in P	The business which faces an elastic demand for its products can decrease prices.	Lower prices. Increased demand. Increased sales revenue.

Determinants of price elasticity of demand

The following are some factors which determine the extent to which a product is price elastic.

√ **The availability of substitutes:** If more substitutes are available, the product is more likely to be sensitive to price changes.

√ **The proportion of consumer income:** The larger the proportion of consumer income spent on the product, the more elastic the product is likely to be.

√ **Time:** The more time consumers have to shift their purchasing patterns, the more price elastic is the demand for the product.

√ **Addiction:** The extent to which consumers are addicted to a product determines its elasticity of demand, e.g., alcohol tends to be an inelastic product for alcoholics.

√ **Perception of the product:** The PED depends on the extent to which the product is perceived as a necessity or luxury. Products which are perceived as necessities, e.g., staples, such as rice, corn and potatoes, have a relatively inelastic demand. That is, even if the price of the product is increased, the quantity demanded is not reduced significantly.

Importance of PED for businesses: Knowledge of price elasticity of demand helps businesses determine their pricing policy and strategy.

Income Elasticity of Demand

Measures the responsiveness of quantity demanded to an increase or decrease in consumers' income alone.

YED = % Change in Quantity demanded
_____
% Change in Income

Question: With an increase in annual income from $10,000 to $11,000, the consumers have increased their demand for rice from 1500 bags to 1600 bags. Using this data, calculate the income elasticity of demand (YED) and comment on your results.

1. Calculate the % change in Quantity Demanded (Δ in **Qd**/Old **Qd**) = 100/1500 = 0.07

2. Calculate the % change in Income (Δ in **Income**/Old **Income**) = 1000/10,000 = 0.1

3. Using the formula YED = **% Change in Quantity demanded** / **% Change in Income** = 0.07/0.1 ➡ 0.7

Interpretation: In this case, the income elasticity for rice is less than 1, implying that rice is a normal good (a necessity) for consumers. We also see that the % change in Qd is less than the % change in income, indicating that rice, in this case, is an income inelastic commodity.

The golden rule for interpreting YED values

YED value	Product classification	Inference
Zero to one	Normal goods, e.g., staples, such as rice, corn, wheat, bread, potatoes and water, are classified as normal goods	The demand for these products does not respond significantly to changes in income.
Greater than one	Luxury goods	An increase in income tends to cause an increase in demand and vice versa.
Less than zero	Inferior goods	An increase in income causes a decrease in demand.

Determinants of income elasticity of demand

The following are some factors which affects the income elasticity of demand:

√ Level of consumer income

√ The extent to which goods are considered as necessities or luxury items

√ Consumers' perception of a firm's product and services

√ State of the economy.

The importance of YED for businesses

1. The values from YED calculations give businesses insights into the nature of their products.

2. Knowledge of income elasticity can be used to gauge consumers' perception of a product.

3 Firms can make use of YED to predict how the state of economic affairs affects the demand for their products and services.

Cross elasticity of demand

An increase or decrease in demand for one product following a change in price of another product alone.

$$XED = \frac{\% \text{ Change in Quantity demanded for product X}}{\% \text{ Change in the price of product Y}}$$

Products that are closely related are classified as either substitutes or complements.

Substitutes (alternative products): The increase in the price of one product results in a fall in the quantity demanded of that product and an increase in the demand for a substitute product. Suppose lamb and beef are substitute products; if the lamb price increases, consumers may opt for beef, thereby increasing the demand for beef.

Complements (products which must be used together): Car and petrol are complements; consequently, an indefinite increase in the price of petrol may lead to a decrease in the demand for cars.

Question: Calculate the cross-elasticity when the price of lamb (Y) increases by 25% and the quantity demanded for beef (X) increases by 40%.

Answer: Applying the formula $XED = \frac{\% \text{ Change in Quantity demanded for product X}}{\% \text{ Change in the price of product Y}}$ ➡ 40/25 = 1.6

Interpretation of the XED values

1. The XED value for substitute goods is positive.

2. The stronger the relationship between the substitutes, the higher is the XED value.

3. The XED value for complementary goods is negative.

4. A zero value indicates that there is no relationship between the quantity demanded of one product and the price of another product.

Determinants of cross elasticity of demand

Generally, two factors determine the cross elasticity of demand:

1. The extent to which products are weak or strong substitutes – **Positive Elasticity**

2. The extent to which two products complement each other – **Negative Elasticity**.

The importance of XED for businesses

Knowledge of cross elasticity of demand helps businesses revise their pricing strategies in response to any change in the prices of their competitor products/services. XED values enable businesses to develop other marketing strategies for promoting their products and drawing customers from rival products. For example, a business may want to strengthen its advertising and promotion against products bearing a branding similar to its own products.

In addition, cross elasticity of demand also helps businesses maximise their revenue and profits by setting appropriate prices for complementary goods.

Advertising elasticity of demand

The change in quantity demanded that results from changes in advertising expenditure.

$$AED = \frac{\% \text{ Change in Quantity demanded}}{\% \text{ Change in advertising expenditure}}$$

Products that are closely related are classified as either substitutes or complements.

Question: A firm increased its advertising expenditure from $2 million to $2.5 million, which increased the demand for its products from 7-million units to 10-million units. Calculate and interpret the advertising elasticity for this firm.

1. Calculate the % Change in Quantity demanded = (Δ in **Qd**/Old **Qd**) ➡ 3/7= 0.43

2. Calculate the % change in advertising expenditure
   (Δ in **Advertising expenditure**/Old **Advertising expenditure**) = 0.5/2 = 0.25

3. Using the formula
   YED = % **Change in Quantity demanded** / % **Change in advertising expenditure** = 0.43/0.25 = 1.72

Interpretation of the AED values

An AED value of 1 or higher indicates a positive relationship between advertising expenditure and quantity demanded. The higher the AED value, the more responsive is the quantity demanded to the change in advertising expenditure. Consequently, negative values suggest the opposite of this relationship.

Determinants of advertising elasticity

√ Sales-revenue objective and profit objectives of the firm

√ Effectiveness of advertising and promotion campaign

√ Funding available for advertising expenditure

The importance of AED

Knowledge of, and application of advertising elasticity helps a firm understand the extent of its advertising expenditure, the effectiveness of its advertising campaign, and the effects these have on the consumer demand for the firm's products.

The relationship between elasticities and the product life cycle

Introduction

Price elasticity: At this stage of the product life cycle, demand will be price inelastic as any change in price is hardly likely to result in a significant increase or decrease in demand.

Income elasticity: is also likely to be low since we can assume that the product is relatively unknown at this stage and any increase in consumers' income is hardly likely to affect quantity demanded.

Cross elasticity: At this stage the relationship with cross elasticity is very much dependent on the extent to which consumers view the product as weak / strong substitutes or necessary complements.

Advertising elasticity: is expected to be low as the product is now being introduced to the market.

Growth

Price elasticity: Is more positive at this stage, because consumers will respond to any change in price by increasing or decreasing the quantity demanded. If the success of the product results in an increase in price, consumers are likely to reduce their demand. On the other hand, increasing competition may push the firm to lower price; hence, consumers are likely to respond by demanding more of the product. However, the extent to which elasticity increases or decreases will depend on the nature of the product.

Income elasticity: The nature of the product will also determine how consumers respond when they experience an increase in income. For example, if the product is a normal good we can expect the relationship at this stage to be one of income inelasticity. On the other hand, if the product is a luxury item then an increase or decrease in quantity demanded will depend on consumers' incomes.

Cross elasticity: At the growth stage we can expect to see some movements with regard to cross elasticity. For example, if the product is established as a substitute to one offered by competitors, then customers will respond to any decrease in price by switching away from competitors' products.

Advertising elasticity: We can assume that the product will be advertised aggressively at this stage. Successful advertising is likely to lead to an increase in advertising elasticity.

Maturity

Price elasticity: At this stage competitors are offering similar products at competitive prices. Price elasticity, therefore, is likely to be high as consumers respond to the firm's adjustment to prices in response to that of its competitors.

Income elasticity: is determined by how much of their extra income consumers are willing to spend on the product or turn to a competing brand.

Cross elasticity: Substitutes are well established in the market at this stage. Competitors' response to the firm's pricing strategy will impact demand for the product. The quantity demanded for the product at this stage is likely to fall if the price of substitutes decreases.

Advertising elasticity: The product is still being marketed aggressively. The need to keep it competitive by employing strategies such as attracting new users might necessitate increasing the advertising budget. Here again, the successful marketing campaign will lead to an increase in demand for the product in relation to any increases or decreases in expenditure associated with advertising.

Decline

Price Elasticity: At this stage as the product is on its way out of the market, the price is reduced in an effort to sell off available stock. The price reduction might result in a short surge in demand; hence, we can conclude that, in this case, price elasticity will increase in the short run.

Income elasticity: If this product is a luxury item customers may be inclined to take advantage of the low price and spend some of their extra income on this product. For the period the product is on sale, this decrease in price may very well lead to a short term reduction in demand for competitors' products.

Advertising expenditure is restricted, yet in the short run the firm is likely to see some increase in the demand for its products at a percentage above that of any decrease in its advertising budget.

The relationship between price elasticity and sales revenue

PED value	Interpretation	Sales revenue
One to infinity	Demand is elastic	Sales revenue is likely to be low unless the firm reduces the price of its products. Reducing the price of a product that is price elastic increases sales revenue.
One	Demand is unitary	No effect on sales revenue irrespective of whether the firm increases or reduces the price of the product.
Zero to one	Demand is inelastic	An inelastic demand indicates that a percentage change in price causes a smaller percentage change in quantity demanded. A firm whose product reflects inelastic demand can raise the price of that product, thereby increasing its sales revenue.

4.5: PROMOTION

Promotion is an element of market mix and involves activities, such as **advertising, public relations, sales promotion** and **direct marketing**. Generally, promotion is used to communicate the information about the other elements of the marketing mix.

The objectives of promotion

√ Creating awareness of the firm's current products or services

√ Introducing new products or services to the market

√ Persuading current and potential consumers to buy products or services

√ Increasing sales revenue and profits

√ Establishing customer loyalty and encouraging repeat purchases

√ Establishing and positioning a brand amongst competing brands

√ Inducing desired buyer behaviour

Types of promotion

Above-the-line promotion

Above-the-line promotion refers to using the mass media to promote products/services. Some of the media are listed below:

√ Television   √ Internet

√ Radio   √ Magazines.

The effectiveness and limitations of some above–the-line promotional tools

Promotional tool	Effectiveness	Limitation
Television	√ Can reach a wide audience √ Creative advertising: sight, sound, motion	√ Relatively expensive √ Minimum time to convey the message
Radio	√ Reasonable/affordable √ Makes effective use of sound and voice	√ The need to advertise with more than one station √ Lacks sight and motion
Internet	√ Extensive/global reach √ Cost-effective and enduring	√ Not trusted by all
Magazines	√ Reaches frequent readers and subscribers √ Various rates and size of advertisements offered	√ Ad space can be very expensive √ Long lead-time: Need to book the ad space in advance

Generally, above-the-line promotion is very effective in attracting large market segments because of the far-reaching capabilities of advertising media such as television, internet, radio and national newspapers. This type of promotion, however, has a number of limitations which include the high costs associated with acquiring advertising space or time.

Below the line promotion

This form of promotion excludes the use of mass media. It includes such techniques as **direct marketing, branding** and **sales promotion**.

The effectiveness and limitations of some below-the-line promotional tools

Direct marketing: Firms target customers directly through the use of media, such as **emails, flyers, brochures** and **coupons**.

Direct marketing techniques focus directly on the target segment and can be considered a flexible approach for multi-product firms. One of the limitations of direct marketing is the high cost associated with the production and distribution of promotional materials.

Sales promotion: A single or a combination of short-term enticements aimed at encouraging customers to increase their purchases. Examples of sales promotion activities include **buy- one- get-one–free offers, competitions, free samples** and **lines of credit at discounted rates**.

Sales promotion techniques facilitate almost-immediate feedback, as in the case of free samples, from customers or potential customers. These techniques, however, are short-term strategies and do not guarantee repeat purchases or customer loyalty.

Branding: This is an act whereby businesses create a distinctive trade mark – name, symbol, jingle, slogans – to distinguish themselves, along with their products or services, from their competitors. As a promotion tool, branding helps create brand loyalty amongst customers. However, creating and maintaining an effective brand is a costly affair.

Factors determining a firm's choice of promotional technique

√ Marketing objectives

√ Consumer-protection legislation

√ The market segment to be targeted

√ Competitors' advertising strategies

√ Cost and appropriateness of the promotional medium

√ The nature of the product and its position in the product life cycle

You must be able to:

1. **Distinguish** between the different types of promotion.
2. **Analyse** the various promotional tools and discuss their effectiveness.

© The IBO, 2007

Promotional mix

A firm's promotional mix represents a combination of above the line and below the line tactics to communicate the merits of its products or services. An effective promotional mix will be geared towards what some market experts call the *AIDA* model:

Attention: Making current and prospective consumers aware of the business's products or services by communicating their benefits.

Interest: Providing information about the products or services to raise the level of consumer response to products or services.

Desire: The promotion of the product or service must stimulate the buying desire in consumers.

Action: The promotional mix must be effective in translating the buying desire into a purchase.

To prepare and implement an effective promotional mix, a firm must be able to integrate advertising, sales promotion, public relations and personal selling tactics.

A health-drink company's promotional mix may include the following:

1. Television commercials
2. Packaging
3. Sales promotion, e.g., discounts
4. Public relations, sponsorship of sports teams.
5. Branding
6. Billboards

You must be able to **prepare** an appropriate promotional mix. © The IBO, 2007

4.6: PLACE (DISTRIBUTION)

This fourth element of the marketing mix relates to the placement and distribution of products or services.

Distribution: The act of facilitating the movement of products from manufacturers to consumers.

Types of distribution channels

A channel of distribution represents a system through which goods and services flow from manufacturers to consumers. Channels of distribution are classified into four levels:

√ One-level channel
√ Two-level channel
√ Three-level channel
√ Four-level channel.

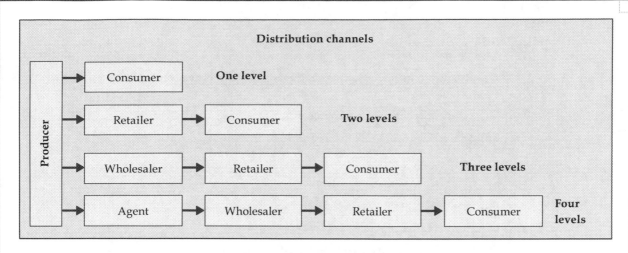

Distribution channels

The effectiveness of the channels of distribution

Channels of distribution	Effectiveness	Limitation
One-level channel – direct marketing	Producer has full control over all aspects of marketing the product/service, e.g., distribution and pricing.	Assuming total responsibility of marketing aspects can be costly for the producer, e.g., warehousing and distribution costs will be higher than normal.
Two-level channel	The retailer eases the marketing pressure for the producer by taking on distribution and other retailing functions.	The producer's profit margin is reduced.
Three-level channel	Wholesalers purchase in bulk and so ease warehousing cost for the producer.	The producer has very little or no control over how the product is marketed.
Four-level channel	The involvement of agents gives producers some control over how their products are marketed.	The distribution process is lengthened; at times, transactions may become cumbersome and bureaucratic.

You must be able to **discuss** the effectiveness of different types of distribution channels. © The IBO, 2007

Elements of the distribution channel

Producers	Agents
√ Manufacturing/creating goods and services	√ Serve as producer's representatives
√ Sourcing raw materials	√ Connect buyers with sellers of products or services
√ Warehousing and distribution	√ Carry out promotional activities on behalf of sellers

Wholesalers

√ Provide market information for the products they stock

√ Finance the production process by paying manufacturers in advance for their products

√ Supplying, warehousing and inventory

√ Bulk purchases and distribution

Retailers

√ Buy products from the wholesaler

√ Offer a wide range of products or services

√ Offer credit facilities to regular, trustworthy customers

√ Display products or services they offer for sale

√ Provide information about the products or services they offer for sale

Some types of retailers

√ Franchisees

√ Dealerships

√ Chain stores

√ Hypermarkets and supermarkets

√ Independent retailers

Distribution strategy

A firm's distribution strategy is an action plan for getting its products or services to target customers. The distribution strategies range from one-level distribution channel (direct marketing) to multi-level distribution channel (the use of one or more intermediaries).

The distribution strategy adopted by a firm is determined by one or more factors:

√ Cost

√ Proximity to customers

√ Nature of the product

√ Marketing objectives

√ Target customers

√ Competitors' distribution strategy.

You must be able to **evaluate** the effectiveness of different types of distribution channels including producers, wholesalers, agents and retailers.

© The IBO, 2007

Supply chain management/Logistics
(HIGHER LEVEL FOCUS)

Supply chain management involves planning, coordinating, executing and controlling the activities associated with the movement of products and services through the channel of distribution. Activities which are associated with supply chain management include a combination of decisions about location, production, transportation, storage, financing, and supplier alignment.

How can organisations increase the efficiency of the supply chain?

√ Developing and implementing a carefully crafted strategy for managing the flow of products, information and finances which are pivotal to the supply chain management process

√ Aligning with reliable suppliers who provide quality products and services at competitive prices and offer flexible and reasonable payment terms

√ Adopting an efficient and reliable stock-management system for ensuring the movement of stock in and out of the business. This includes managing the inventory of products received from suppliers and the stock of finished or unfinished products.

√ Ensuring total quality in the production process

√ Maintaining efficient transport and other delivery systems

√ Providing relevant training to the teams handling various aspects of the supply chain

√ Developing and implementing systems to monitor the performance of the supply chain

You must be able to **examine** how organisations can increase the efficiency of the supply chain.

© The IBO, 2007

4.7: INTENATIONAL MARKETING

International marketing is about selling goods and services across international boundaries.

Entry into international markets – Why?

√ To boost the sales volume and revenue

√ To capture new markets

√ To take advantage of opportunities in international markets

√ To ease competitive pressure from rivals in the local market

Entry into international markets: Possible strategies

√ Joint ventures

√ Strategic alliances

√ License agreements

√ Mergers and acquisitions

√ Direct Foreign Investments

√ Franchising

√ Exporting

Entry into international markets: Opportunities

√ Increase market share

√ Gain international recognition for the company and its brand

√ Increase revenue and profit

√ Benefit from economies of scale

√ Benefit from favourable Government business legislation

Entry into international markets: Threats

Political: Government legislation which may be unfavourable to international business, high taxes and tariffs, unstable political situations, no legal protection for patents and copyrights

Economic: High rate of inflation, high level of unemployment, slow or negative economic growth

Socio-cultural: Negative views of international businesses, cultural habits, language, religious beliefs, unethical business practices

Technological: International companies who seek to market their goods and services to developing countries may be constrained by the non-availability of or inadequate technical resources, e.g., poor ICT infrastructure, inefficient postal services, lack of people with relevant technical expertise.

You must be able to **evaluate** the opportunities and threats posed by entry into international markets.

© The IBO, 2007

The cultural, legal, political, social and economic issues of entering international markets
(HIGHER LEVEL FOCUS)

Cultural issues

√ Language

√ Religion

√ Work and business ethics

√ Values and norms

√ Habits and preferences

Legal issues

√ Patent and copyright legislation

√ Consumer-protection legislation

√ Employee legislation

√ Discrimination legislation

√ Business legislation

Political issues

√ Political relationship between countries

√ Political stability

√ Taxes, tariffs, quotas, subsidies

√ Efficiency of government ministries

√ Government policies regarding business regulations

Economic issues

√ Level of unemployment

√ Level of inflation

√ Exchange rate

√ Spending pattern of the average consumer

√ Standard of living

√ Economic growth and development

Social issues

√ Education of the workforce

√ Growth or decline in the population

√ Expectations of how businesses should execute their social responsibilities

√ The activities and influence of NGOs and pressure groups

√ Level of poverty and crime

You must be able to **analyse** given situations considering the cultural, legal, political, social and economic issues of entering international markets.

© The IBO, 2007

4.8: E-COMMERCE

E-commerce is about conducting business transactions online.

Some e-commerce activities

√ Trading in equities

√ Making hotel reservations via the Internet

√ Wholesale and retail shopping via the Internet

√ Booking flight tickets

√ Sourcing suppliers

√ Online banking transactions

E-commerce: Business to Business (B2B)

In e-commerce, B2B refers to online transactions between businesses only. B2B transactions involve exchange of goods, services and information via the Internet. Examples of B2B transactions.

√ Exchange of quotations between businesses

√ Supply chain management

√ Corporate banking transactions

√ Cataloguing of goods and services

√ Sourcing goods and services

E-commerce: Business to Consumer (B2C)

In e-commerce, B2C refers to online business transactions between businesses and customers. Unlike B2B, B2C facilitates retail transactions only. Examples of B2C transactions:

√ Online banking

√ Payment of utility bills

√ Purchase of products, e.g., books from www.amazon.com.

The effects of e-commerce on the marketing mix

Product/service

√ Information about the firm's products/services is readily available.

√ Products can be customised to meet specific needs, e.g., Dell allows customers to personalise laptops or desktops they purchase.

√ Customer support and after-sale services are readily available via FAQs and help-desk services.

√ Self-service is facilitated as customers can choose from the range of products and services which are displayed on the firm's website.

NOTE: Products which are sold via the Internet take on some level of intangibility. Therefore, the marketing strategy for such products must address this limitation by providing adequate information about the products. Marketers suggest that one strategy to overcome intangibility is to create a strong brand image for the product.

Price

√ Selling a product via the Internet reduces the cost associated with personnel and infrastructure; this reduction in cost allows for products and services to be priced competitively.

√ Changes in prices can be communicated almost immediately.

√ Various methods of online payment for goods and services are available.

√ Penetration pricing strategies can be used to facilitate demand.

√ Price bundling is also a typical strategy adopted by firms selling their products/services online.

√ Customers can browse the Internet for the best deals.

√ Returning customers are given the added advantage of price discounts.

NOTE: When setting the price of its products, firms consider their customer base, the level of demand and their capacity to deal with increases in online orders.

Place

√ Orders are facilitated online, but the distribution process is supported via national and international postal systems and courier services, such as DHL and FedEx.

√ Warehousing and distribution functions are sometimes outsourced.

√ Companies which sell digital products, e.g., software and eBooks, reduce their costs significantly as there is no need for storage or intermediaries in the distribution process. This also shortens the chain of distribution. Additionally, customers can purchase some non-digital products directly from the manufacturer, via online orders.

Promotion

Internet advertising facilitates direct-marketing strategies, which include use of solicited or unsolicited emails and online banners. Also, traditional promotional strategies (such as discounts, rebates and free gifts) can be communicated to existing and prospective customers.

You must be able to **analyse** the effect of e-commerce on the marketing mix.   © The IBO, 2007

The cost and benefits of e-commerce

For the organisation

Costs	Benefits
√ High initial-setup costs, e.g., security	√ Reduction in costs, e.g., distribution
√ Poor technology can prove to be costly	√ Global market reach – more customers
√ No option for accepting cash payments	√ 24/7 presence
√ Charges from credit-card companies	√ Ability to compete with larger firms
√ Competitive online firms	√ Increased sales revenue and profits

For consumers

Costs	Benefits
√ Likelihood of fraud	√ 24-hour access to the business
√ Fee associated with use of credit instruments	√ Convenient shopping: Anywhere, anytime
√ Number of transactions is limited by the use of credit instruments	√ Instant confirmation of transactions
	√ Availability of bargain prices

You must be able to **discuss** the costs and benefits of e-commerce to firms and consumers.   © The IBO, 2007

5.1: METHODS OF PRODUCTION

Method	Some features	Some applications
Job	Employs simple or advanced technology Functional group of equipment and staff	Small and large businesses One-off jobs, e.g., building a house
Batch	Division of labour and specialisation Goods are produced in batches	Bakery Software industry
Line and Flow	Highly mechanised and automated Goods are produced in a continuous stream	The manufacturing industry, e.g., car manufacturing
Mass	Capital intensive Production of standardised outputs	Food-canning plant Printing plant

Method	Advantages	Disadvantages
Job	Flexibility and motivation Closer supervision of work	Products are very expensive No economies of scale
Batch	Labour specialisation Economies of scale	Monotonous tasks High levels of work-in-progress
Line and Flow	High level of productivity Less dependence on manual labour	Warehousing may raise storage costs
Mass	Economies of scale Rapid production	Expensive due to heavy capital investment and maintenance

You must be able to **describe** and **compare** the features and application of each method of production.

© The IBO, 2007

Cell production and teamwork
(HIGHER LEVEL FOCUS)

Cell production: People and machinery are grouped into cells (teams). Each cell is headed by a leader, and the whole cell takes responsibility for major aspects of production (for example, product design and quality control).

Cell Production: Productivity implications
(HIGHER LEVEL FOCUS)

Advantages	Disadvantages
√ Improvement in quality and productivity	√ Conflict amongst teams
√ Greater motivation	√ Poor performance of team affects others
√ Shared commitment to a common goal	√ Work restricted to the pace of the slowest worker
√ Flexibility due to multitasking	

Implications of changing the production system

(HIGHER LEVEL FOCUS)

The following are some of the factors to be considered before making a decision to change production system:

- √ Sources and availability of funding
- √ Level of demand for the firm's product
- √ Cost, e.g., cost associated with training, maintenance, downsizing the workforce.
- √ Employees' resistance
- √ Suppliers of the technology
- √ Effects on the environment

Implications for marketing

Some of the implications for marketing are:

Product: Changes in quantity, quality, design, usage

Price: Changes in pricing strategies

Place: Changes in distribution strategies - distribution channels

Promotion: Changes in advertising and promotional strategies.

Implications for human resources

Some of the implications for human resources are:

Training: New and/or existing employees

Recruitment: Recruiting additional or specialist employees

Redundancy: Adopting mechanised and automated systems may result in downsizing

Remuneration and other benefits: May be increased or decreased.

Implications for finance

Some of the implications for finance are:

- √ Cost of investment
- √ Sources of funding
- √ Maintenance and replacement costs
- √ Interest payments.

You must be able to **analyse** the implications for marketing, human resource management and finance that arise from changing the production system.

© The IBO, 2007

The need for organisations to use multiple production systems

The following factors influence the extent to which a business will employ multiple production systems:

- √ The nature of the organisation
- √ The types of goods produced
- √ Customer requirements
- √ The cost of operating multiple systems.

You must be able to **understand** the need for organisations to use more than one method of production.

© The IBO, 2007

5.2: COSTS AND REVENUE

Costs: The expenditure incurred due to a business activity.

Revenue: The income generated from a business activity before expenses associated with the activity are deducted.

Types of costs

Cost	Definition	Examples
Fixed Cost (FC)	A cost which remains the same irrespective of the level of output	Rent, interest rates, managers' salaries
Variable Cost (VC)	A cost which changes with the level of business activity or output	Raw materials, piece-rate wages, utilities
Semi-variable	A cost which reflects both fixed and variable elements	Wages with overtime payments, electricity charges
Direct/Prime	Costs which are directly associated with, and can be traced back to, a specific business activity or level of output	Direct material Direct labour Direct expenses
Indirect/Overheads	Costs which are incurred for the joint benefit of a range of business activities and are not directly related to a given level of output	Indirect material, e.g., petrol Indirect labour, e.g., salaries Indirect expenses, e.g., taxes

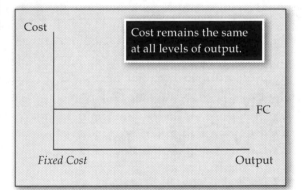

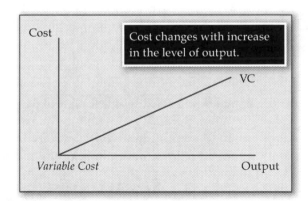

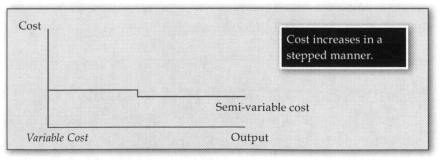

Cost formulae

Total, Average and Marginal costs

1. Total Cost **(TC)** = Total Fixed Cost (TFC) + Total Variable Cost (TVC)

2. Average Cost **(AC)** = Total Cost (TC)/Quantity (Q)

3. Average Variable Cost **(AVC)** = Total Variable Cost (TVC)/Output (Q)

4. Average Fixed Cost **(AFC)** = Total Fixed Cost (TFC)/Output (Q)

5. Marginal Cost **(MC)** = $\dfrac{\text{Change in Total Cost}}{\text{Change in quantity}}$ = $\Delta TC / \Delta Q$

Revenue

Revenue refers to the income generated from the sale of a given level of output during a specific period.

A firm's sources of revenue relate to the nature of the business activities it conducts. Some possible sources of revenue are:

√ Sales   √ Donations   √ Commissions   √ Loans   √ Royalties   √ Grants.

Revenue formulae

Total, Average and Marginal Revenue and Profit

1. Total Revenue **(TR)** = Total Quantity sold (Q) x Average Price (P)

2. Average Revenue **(AR)** = Total Revenue (TR)/Quantity Sold (Q)

3. Marginal Revenue **(MR)** = $\Delta TR / \Delta Q$

4. **Profit** = Total Revenue (TR) – Total Cost (TC)

You must be able to:

1. **Define, explain** and **give examples** of each different type of cost.

2. **Explain** the meaning of revenue.

3. **Comment** on possible sources of revenue.

© The IBO, 2007

Contribution to fixed costs

Contribution refers to the amount of revenue, per product or level of business activity, which is available to pay fixed costs and provide a profit after variable costs have been deducted.

Total Contribution = Sales Revenue – Variable Cost

Or

Unit Contribution = Selling Price per Unit – Variable Cost per Unit (P – AVC)

Profit = Total Contribution – Fixed Cost

Question

Caribbean Foods Ltd. produced and sold 20,000 bottles of sugarcane juice. Each bottle of juice was sold at $10.00. The variable cost per bottle of juice is $3.00. Calculate the contribution per bottle of juice to fixed cost.

Unit Contribution

Since contribution per unit = Selling price per unit – variable cost per unit

Selling price per unit = $10.00

Variable cost per unit = $ 3.00

Therefore, unit contribution = $10.00 – $3.00 = $7.00

Interpretation: Each bottle of cane juice contributed $7.00 to fixed cost.

Total Contribution

Total Contribution = Total Sales Revenue – Total Variable Cost

Therefore: (20,000 x $10.00) - (20,000 x $3.00) = $200,000 - $60,000 = $140,000.

Interpretation: 20,000 bottles of cane juice contributed $140,000 to the total fixed cost of production.

Reminder

Contribution is *not* profit; profit is accounted for after **fixed** and **variable costs** are **deducted** from **sales revenue**.

Profit = Contribution – Fixed Cost

Generally, cost and profit centres are used by firms to determine the cost incurred and the profit generated from activities or departments. Cost and profit centres help the firm to identify how various aspects of its operation contribute to its financial stability.

You must be able to **explain** and calculate contribution to fixed costs.

Cost and profit centres
(HIGHER LEVEL FOCUS)
The nature of cost and profit centres

Cost centres: These are specific areas or activities within the firm to which costs are attributed, e.g., departments, product line, geographic area, equipment, business functions.

Profit centres: These are areas of the business which are operated with the sole intent of generating profits. A profit centre can be associated with any aspect of the firm's business activity, e.g., products, machine, departments, branch.

Value of cost and profit centres to a firm

√ Help measure and monitor the cost and financial returns for each business activity

√ Facilitate financial planning and control

√ Define a clear financial structure for the organisation

√ Foster teamwork

(Contd...)

Some limitations of cost and profit centres

√ May be difficult to allocate costs to, or associate profit with, some activities

√ Employees may be constrained by the management's expectations of controlling costs and generating profits across cost and profit centres

√ Consider only financial matrices and largely ignore issues, such as the contribution of intangible assets

You must be able to:

1. **Explain** the nature of cost and profit centres.

2. **Analyse** the value of cost and profit centres to a firm.

© The IBO, 2007

Contribution analysis
Caribbean Traders Ltd.

Particulars	Tables ($)	Chairs ($)	Beds ($)	Total ($)
Sales Revenue	125,000	300,000	100,000	525,000
Total Variable Cost (TVC)	60,000	195,000	93,500	348,500
Contribution	65,000	105,000	6,500	176,500
Fixed Cost (FC)	12,000	20,000	10,000	42,000
Profit	53,000	85,000	(3,500)	134,500

Based on the analysis, the management of Caribbean Traders Ltd. intends to drop beds from its product mix. However, before taking such a decision, management should consider a number of factors which include:

1. Beds contribute $6,500, which helps recover the fixed cost of $10,000

2. The company will continue to incur a fixed cost of $10,000 even after dropping beds

3. The total profit of $134,000 will be reduced by $6,500

4. Competitors will get an opportunity to increase their market share

5. Customers who want to purchase tables, chairs and beds together may consider other vendors

6. There is the possibility that the demand for beds may increase in the future.

The role of contribution analysis
(HIGHER LEVEL FOCUS)

As a decision making tool, contribution analysis is useful under the following circumstances:

√ When faced with the decision to make or buy a product

√ When faced with the decision to drop or retain a product

√ When faced with outsourcing decisions

√ To analyse the company's product mix (Portfolio)

√ To develop pricing strategies – contribution pricing strategy

√ To determine the break-even level of output

√ For special-order decisions

√ To compare competing strategies.

You must be able to **analyse** the role of contribution analysis in determining the viability of each product for a multi-product firm.

© The IBO, 2007

5.3: BREAK-EVEN ANALYSIS

Break-even is the level of business activity where the total revenue earned from that activity is the same as its total cost. Break-even analysis examines the relationship between changes in cost and volume and how such changes affect profit.

Break-even Point ⟹ **TR = TC**

Methods of break-even analysis

Problem: A company makes a product which is sold for $25.00 each. The variable cost of production per unit is $5.00, and the total fixed cost is $20,000 at an expected level of production of 10,000 units.

Required: Use *quantitative* and *graphical* methods to calculate **break-even quantity (BEQ)**, **profit** and **margin of safety**.

The quantitative methods

Using the contribution rule	Using the Total Cost (TC) = Total Revenue (TR) rule
Break-even quantity = Fixed Cost/Contribution per unit	**Break-even quantity:** Total Cost = Total Revenue
Contribution per unit = Selling price – Variable cost per unit	$20,000+\$5Q = \$25Q$
$25.00 - \$5.00 = \$20.00$	$20,000 = \$25Q - \$5Q$
BEQ = 20,000/\$20 = 1000 units	$20,000 = \$20Q$
	BEQ = $20,000/\$20 = 1000$ units

Profit

Profit = Total Revenue (TR) – Total Cost (TC)

$250,000 - $70,000 = $180,000

Margin of safety =Expected level of output – Break-even quantity

10,000 – 1000 = 9000 units

Margin of safety: This represents the difference between expected level of activity and breakeven units. More specifically, the margin of safety represents the extent to which output can fall short of targeted levels before a loss can be incurred.

The graphical method

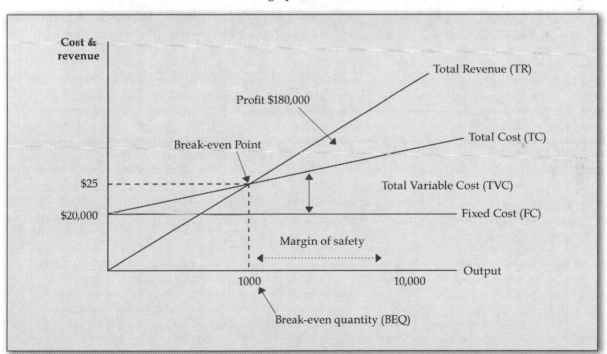

Change in break-even
(HIGHER LEVEL EXTENSION)

The impact of increase in price

√ The total revenue increases.

√ The total-revenue curve shifts to the left of original curve.

√ The business achieves break-even at a lower level of output.

√ The margin of safety increases.

The impact of increase in fixed and variable costs

√ Increase in fixed cost increases the total cost. Hence, the total-cost curve shifts upwards.

√ The break-even level of output increases.

√ The margin of safety decreases.

> You must be able to **use** quantitative and graphical methods to **analyse** the effects of changes in price or cost on break-even quantity, profit and margin of safety. **(HL Only)**
>
> © The IBO, 2007

Using the break-even formulae to calculate the targeted profit or revenue
(HIGHER LEVEL FOCUS)
Break-even formula

Formula	When it should be used
Fixed Cost / Contribution per unit	To determine the break-even quantity
Fixed Cost / Contribution per unit x Selling Price	To determine the break-even sales revenue
Fixed Cost x Sales Value	Product mix: Sales revenue to break-even
Fixed Cost + Target Profit / Contribution per unit	To determine the output level that is required to achieve the targeted profit
Fixed Cost + Targeted Profit x Selling Price / Contribution per unit	To determine the sales revenue that must be generated to achieve the targeted profit
Total Cost / Output	To determine the break-even price

Assumptions and limitations of break-even analysis
(HIGHER LEVEL FOCUS)

Assumptions

√ Costs and revenues increase only because of an increase in output and sales.

√ Costs are divided into fixed and variable components.

√ Total revenue and total cost behave in a linear manner.

√ Selling price, fixed costs and variable costs per unit are constant.

√ The analysis covers a single product; if there is a product mix, it assumes that the mix is constant.

√ The state of technology and production facilities is static.

√ All the produced goods/services will be sold.

Limitations

√ Fixed costs are accounted for over a limited range of activity.

√ In case of changing product mix with different profit margins, it is difficult to determine the volume which should be sold to achieve optimal profit.

√ Closing stock carried over to the next accounting period does not contain components of fixed costs.

√ The analysis does not consider the impact of qualitative factors on the volume and level of business activity.

You must be able to **analyse** the assumptions and limitations of break-even analysis. © The IBO, 2007

5.4: QUALITY ASSURANCE

Quality is a subjective concept. Therefore, quality products or services fulfil the needs of the customers for whom they are intended.

Some dimensions of quality

Quality control and quality assurance

Quality control

Quality control is the process of ensuring that a firm's products/services meet certain verifiable characteristics.

Quality-control techniques

√ Sampling   √ Testing

√ Checklists   √ Inspection

Quality assurance

Quality assurance is the act of employing methods and processes which guarantee customers that the quality of products and/or services is consistent.

Dr. Edward Deming outlined the process of quality assurance as follows:

1. **Plan:** Identify specific problem associated with quality and develop action plan for improvement

2. **Do:** Implement the plan

3. **Check:** Evaluate outcomes

4. **Act:** Make changes to the process as necessary. Institutionalise the change.

Some benefits of quality control and quality assurance:

√ Increases customer confidence

√ Gives an edge over competitors

√ Reduces the amount of defective products

√ Enhances company credibility, image, work process and efficiency.

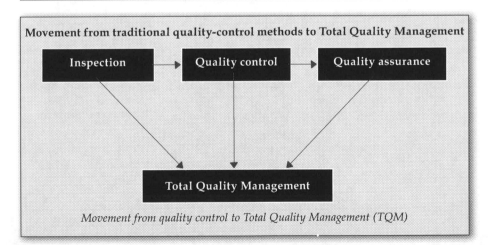

Movement from traditional quality-control methods to Total Quality Management

Movement from quality control to Total Quality Management (TQM)

You must be able to **analyse** the move from traditional quality-control methods to Total Quality Management.

Total Quality Management (TQM)/Total Quality Culture (TQC)

Total Quality Management: "Managing the entire organisation so that it excels in all dimensions of products and service that are important to the customer" (Chase, Aquilano & Jacobs, 2002).

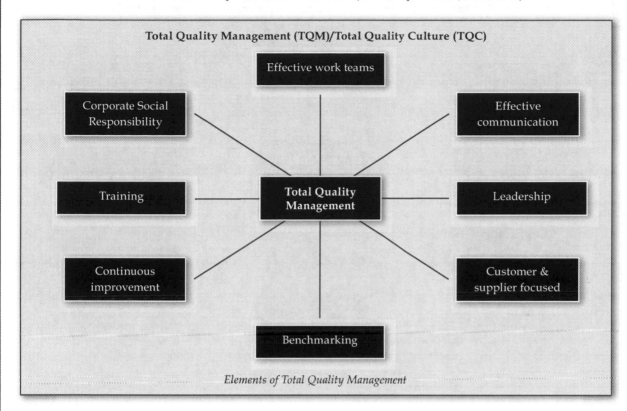

Total Quality Management (TQM)/Total Quality Culture (TQC)

- Effective work teams
- Corporate Social Responsibility
- Effective communication
- Training
- Total Quality Management
- Leadership
- Continuous improvement
- Customer & supplier focused
- Benchmarking

Elements of Total Quality Management

Benefits and limitations of Total Quality Management (TQM)

Benefits

- √ Reduction of defects
- √ Continuous improvement in processes, products and services
- √ Quality products and services
- √ Customer satisfaction
- √ Reduction in average operational cost due to improved efficiency

Limitations

- √ Implementing TQM is a costly exercise
- √ If management and employees are not fully committed, the TQM process will fail
- √ Employees' performance is a function of the system
- √ The implementation involves much bureaucracy

Lean production: This is about maximising efficiency by eliminating waste, reducing bureaucracy, and speeding up the operational process.

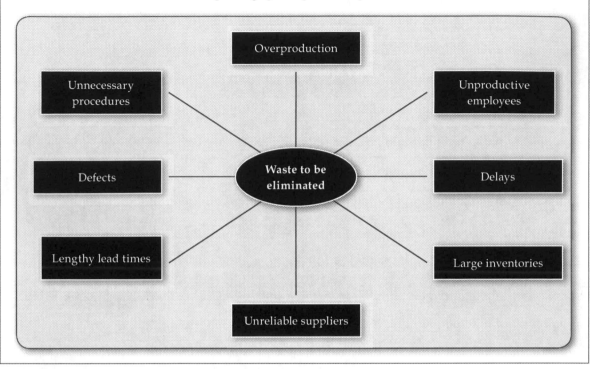

Features of lean production

√ Flexibility at low cost and good customer service

√ Use of few resources – labour, premises, time, tools, etc.

√ Development of close relationship with contractors, suppliers, retailers and customers

√ Customer focus- Lean production puts the customer first

√ Capital rationalisation

√ Continuous improvement – improvements in quality are ongoing

Some benefits of lean production

√ Small inventory

√ Waste minimization

√ Lower cost of production/operation

√ Smaller, effective and productive workforce

Continuous improvement: Kaizen
(HIGHER LEVEL FOCUS)

Kaizen means continuous improvement. It is a system where all employees are given the opportunity to suggest improvements relating to any aspect of the organisation. The Kaizen concept and practice are about making small changes on a regular basis.

The role of Kaizen in quality improvement

√ Right from the Chief Executive Officer to the lowest ranked employee, everyone is involved.

√ It encourages and facilitates gradual improvements in areas, such as work systems, procedures, technology, office layout and production systems.

√ It is an ongoing improvement process.

√ Suggestions for improvements are often driven by quality circles.

You must be able to **explain** the role of Kaizen in quality improvement. © The IBO, 2007

Benchmarking
(HIGHER LEVEL FOCUS)

Benchmarking is a process by which businesses compare and measure their performance against other businesses which are deemed to be excellent practitioners in the industry.

Steps in the benchmarking process

1. Identify what is to be benchmarked.

2. Identify competitors who are regarded as outstanding practitioners within the industry.

3. Decide on the best possible way to gather information – primary and secondary research.

4. Conduct research.

5. Analyse the data gathered from the research to determine where the business's performance is falling short when compared with its competitors.

6. Determine the standards which must be achieved and how they will be achieved.

7. Communicate and seek support for the proposed changes.

8. Implement the decision.

9. Monitor and evaluate.

Advantages of benchmarking

√ Continuous improvement

√ Improvement of quality

√ Organisational change

√ Cost effective

Disadvantages of benchmarking

√ Weaknesses of the firm are exposed to competitors.

√ It is a time-consuming process.

√ The organisation being benchmarked may be unwilling to share its practice.

You must be able to **evaluate** different approaches to quality improvement. © The IBO, 2007

National and international quality standards
(HIGHER LEVEL FOCUS)

Quality standards are the framework and benchmark for effectiveness with regard to how a business meets set national and international criteria relating to the goods/services it offers.

The role of local and national standards in assuring quality
(HIGHER LEVEL FOCUS)

√ Provide a distinctive mark of quality with international recognition

√ Provide customers with an assurance of the quality of the firm's products and or services

√ Reduce production cost and increase customer satisfaction

√ Ensure continuous improvement

√ Ensure effective planning and innovative business activities

Some examples of national and international quality standard organisations
(HIGHER LEVEL FOCUS)

1. The International Organisation for Standardisation (ISO)

2. The Asia Pacific Quality Organisation (IAPQA)

3. The American Society for Quality (ASQ)

4. Airport Council International (ACI)

5. The Council of International Schools (CIS)

You must be able to **explain** the role of local and international standards in assuring quality for customers.

5.5: LOCATION

One of the most important considerations for the management of a firm is where to set up its business operation. Finding the most appropriate location for setting up a business is vital to the success of any business.

Reasons for location: Domestically and internationally

Some of the reasons why businesses choose a specific geographical location are:

√ To take advantage of local or international government incentives, e.g., tax holidays

√ Lower cost of production, e.g., to take advantage of a relatively large and cheap labour pool and other resources

√ Easier access to vital markets

√ Less stringent business legislation.

Consequences of domestic and international locations

Setting up a business in domestic or international locations has both positive and negative consequences. Some of them are listed below:

√ **Political consequences:** e.g., lenient or stricter business legislation

√ **Economic consequences:** e.g., increased inward foreign direct investment, some businesses may be forced to close down because of competition

√ **Social consequences:** e.g., higher standards of living, unemployment as businesses move from one geographic location to another

√ **Technological:** e.g., technology transfers, unemployment.

Causes of domestic/international relocation

Business relocation refers to a management's decision to move the entire business operation from one geographic location to another. Potential causes of relocation are:

√ Increased operational cost, e.g., cost of labour, taxes, raw materials, transportation

√ Shortage of skilled workers

√ Need to expand existing plant facilities

√ Change in government business legislation

√ To capture new markets.

Disadvantages of domestic/international relocation

A number of disadvantages are associated with relocating a business operation.

√ Cost is one of the major disadvantages of relocation. Some relocation costs include setup costs, compensation to workers made redundant, taxes and other costs associated with disposing assets.

√ Relocating a business may lead to loss of valuable customers and loyal and committed employees.

√ Relocated businesses are faced with new challenges, such as labour legislation, language barriers, culture and work habits.

√ If relocation is not carefully planned and executed, an otherwise well-established business can fail.

NOTE: To avoid relocation, some businesses consider activities, such as merging with or acquiring similar firms, subcontracting, leasing and outsourcing. Some businesses also engage in joint ventures and strategic alliances.

Factors influencing the local and international location/relocation of businesses

Political factors: Government stability, favourable business legislation, local, national and international government legislation, free-trade zones.

Economic factors: Cost and availability of raw materials and labour, status of exchange and interest rates, industrial inertia, proximity and availability of markets and customers, government economic incentives.

Social factors: Demographics of the labour population, ethical considerations, life styles, availability of, or the ease of establishing, recreational facilities and activities, quality of labour.

Technological factors: The ease with which technology can be transferred, availability of technological infrastructure such as the Internet.

You must be able to **explain** the causes and consequences of location and relocation, both domestically and internationally.

The impact of globalisation on location
(HIGHER LEVEL FOCUS)

Globalisation has both positive and negative impact on the location of business operations.

Some of the unfavourable effects of globalisation are:

√ Language and cultural barriers

√ Economic trading blocs, e.g., the North American Free Trade Agreement (NAFTA) and the European Union (EU) make it difficult for businesses from non-member countries to trade within these regions

√ Globalisation recognises the need for businesses to be ethically and socially responsible, thereby increasing their operational costs.

You must be able to **consider** the effects of globalisation on location.   © The IBO, 2007

The impact of location/relocation on the functional areas of a business

Functional Area	Impact of location/relocation
Finance	√ Cost of investing in the location, e.g., capital equipment √ Taxes, import and export duties √ Cost of Corporate Social Responsibility initiatives √ Returns on investment
Human Resources	√ Recruitment of suitable workers √ Relocation of existing workers (for example, senior managers) √ Labour and training cost √ Redundancy payments, negotiations with trade unions
Marketing	√ Market segmentation in the new location √ Competitors, if any, and their share of the market √ Opportunities for developing a strong marketing network √ Suitability of the product to the market √ Marketing strategies to be employed
Production	√ Supplier alignment √ Research and development √ Production method: One or multiple √ Quality maintenance and control

You must be able to **analyse** the impact of location of different areas of business activity.

© The IBO, 2007

5.6: INNOVATION
(HIGHER LEVEL FOCUS)

"Innovation is the specific instrument of entrepreneurship, the act that endows resources with new capacity to create wealth."
- Peter Drucker

Innovation, therefore, is about a business staying ahead of its competitors by successfully exploiting, developing and executing new ideas in all areas of its operation.

Types of innovation

√ **Incremental innovation:** Existing products, services, procedures are modified. For example, adjusting an existing marketing strategy.

√ **Radical innovation:** As the name suggests, this is about completely changing existing products, services or practices.

A business can be innovative in a number of areas:

√ Production methods

√ Technology

√ Product development

√ Goods and services offered for sale.

√ Marketing methods

√ Approach to decision making

√ Training methods

Some benefits of innovation
(HIGHER LEVEL EXTENSION)

√ Drives profitable and sustainable business growth

√ Facilitates differentiation and market leadership

√ Establishes corporate image

√ Fosters a culture of research and development

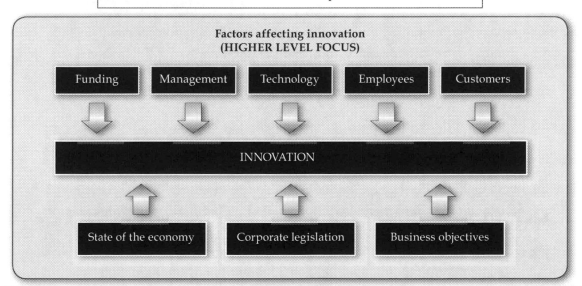

Factors affecting innovation
(HIGHER LEVEL FOCUS)

You must be able to **analyse** the factors affecting innovation.   © The IBO, 2007

Research and development
(HIGHER LEVEL FOCUS)

The importance of research and development for a business

√ Secures the future for the business

√ Ensures competitive edge

√ Leads to improvements in quality and variety of goods and services

√ Attracts external funding

√ Enhances work procedures, processes and employee motivation

√ Establishes crucial business partnerships, such as joint ventures and strategic alliances

You must be able to **explain** the importance of R&D for businesses © The IBO, 2007

Patents, copyrights and trademarks: Intellectual-property rights
(HIGHER LEVEL FOCUS)

INTELLECTUAL-PROPERTY RIGHTS

Patents
These are exclusive legal rights on inventions, e.g., a person who creates a distinct procedure, equipment, or machine can have the invention protected under the patents act.

Copyrights
These are exclusive rights to published works, e.g., books, works of art, music.

Trademarks
Signs or symbols, sound, colour that are used by firms to distinguish themselves from their competitors.

The importance of intellectual-property rights for a business

√ Provide protection against copyright, patent and trademark infringement

√ Encourage and promote creativity and competition

√ Establish customer loyalty, image and brand recognition

You must be able to **explain** the role and **importance** of intellectual-property rights for a business.

© The IBO, 2007

5.7: PRODUCTION PLANNING

Stock control

Stock control is a systematic method of recording, monitoring and reporting the movement of stock, that is, raw materials and components, finished and partly finished goods (work-in-progress), throughout the firm.

Stock levels are determined by the following factors:

√ **Cost.** For example, storage, lighting, heating, security, opportunity costs

√ **Nature of the product.** For example, a firm will be very cautious with the stock levels for perishable goods

√ **Reliability of suppliers**

√ **Nature of the business.** For example, some large manufacturers reduce their inventory levels by adopting a just-in-time approach to their stock management

√ **Unforeseen demand.** For example, some businesses hold extra stock just-in-case of an unexpected increase in demand.

Cost of holding too much stock

√ Storage	√ Spoilage
√ Possible cash flow problem	√ Theft
√ Obsolescence	

Cost of holding too little stock

√ Loss of sales revenue

√ Inability to address sudden increase in demand

√ Customers will turn to competitors

Just-In-Case and Just-In-Time stock control methods

Just-in-case

Just-In-Case is the practice of ordering extra stock, or purchasing, leasing or renting additional storage space to store extra products to meet unexpected increases in demand and other unforeseen circumstances.

Advantages

√ Increased revenue from sales, in case of a surge in demand.

√ Customer loyalty, as business can be relied upon for certain essential products.

√ *Safety net* in stock: When suppliers fall short, the extra stock serves as a buffer.

Disadvantages

√ Increased cost, e.g., for extra stock and storage

√ Money tied up in stock could have been invested in an alternative venture.

Just-in-time

Just-in-time refers to the supply of stock *just in time* for its immediate use. This method helps reduce the costs associated with holding stock.

Advantages	Disadvantages
√ Reduction in costs, e.g., handling and storage costs	√ Inability to take advantage of purchasing economies
√ Waste, theft and obsolescence less likely	√ Late supplies can lead to disruptions and financial losses
√ Greater efficiency in use of materials	√ Possibility of increase in delivery costs

You must be able to **explain** the difference between Just-in-case and Just-in-time stock control. © The IBO, 2007

Traditional stock control
(HIGHER LEVEL FOCUS)

The need for optimum stock levels

A firm must maintain optimum stock levels for the same reasons which are associated with holding too little stock in the inventory. The following are some of the advantages of maintaining an optimum stock level:

√ Ensures that enough goods are available to meet the current demand or a sudden surge in demand

√ Avoids workflow disruptions resulting from shortage of materials

√ Ensures the likelihood of positive contributions to fixed costs

√ Strengthens customers' confidence in the firm's ability to meet their demands, enhancing their commitment to the firm

√ Reduces the costs associated with frequent purchases of stock.

You must be able to **recognise** the need for optimum stock levels. © The IBO, 2007

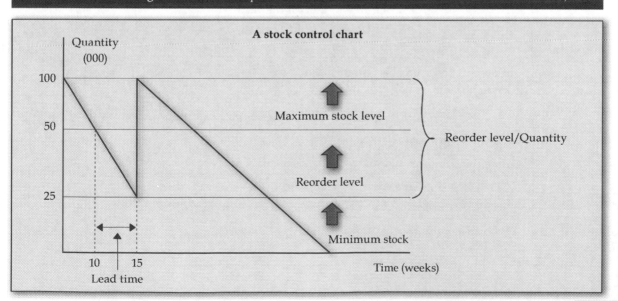

A stock control chart

√ **Maximum stock level:** This is the highest level of stock the business wishes to hold at any point of time.

√ **Reorder stock level:** This is the level to which stock is allowed to fall before it is replenished.

√ **Minimum level of stock:** This is also referred to as buffer or safety stock. This is the level of stock which keeps the business secure in case of delays in delivery or a sudden surge in demand.

√ **Lead time:** This is the time between ordering and replenishing stocks.

√ **Reorder quantity:** The quantity of stock which must be reordered to achieve the maximum stock level.

You must be able to:

1. **Prepare** and **analyse** appropriate graphs.

2. **Explain** different stock control methods and the appropriateness of each method in a given situation.

© The IBO, 2007

Capacity utilisation

Capacity utilisation refers to the percentage of a company's productive capacity which is actually used over a period of time. Capacity utilisation is measured by using the following formula:

Capacity Utilisation = Output/Maximum capacity x 100

Some of the consequences of operating at full capacity are as follows:

√ Fixed cost is spread over a wider level of activities, reducing unit fixed cost

√ Employees' job security is boosted

√ In the long run, the performance of workers and machinery is affected, resulting in absenteeism, breakdowns, and increased maintenance costs.

Outsourcing and subcontracting
(HIGHER LEVEL FOCUS)

Outsourcing and subcontracting are the processes of employing outside agents to perform functions which are normally carried out within the business.

Arguments in favour of outsourcing and subcontracting

√ Business can focus on core activities.

√ Less capital expenditure and reduced operational costs.

√ Outsourcing/subcontracting creates employment.

√ Business is able to meet changing demands.

√ Access to professional expertise and advanced technology.

(Contd...)

Arguments against outsourcing/subcontracting

√ Business may lose control over the project.

√ Outsourcing/subcontracting creates unemployment.

√ Threat to confidentiality is possible.

√ Lack of customer focus as subcontractors are mostly concerned with the viability of the contract.

√ Outsourcing/subcontracting encourages unfair exploitation of human resources.

You must be able to:

1. **Explain** outsourcing and subcontracting.

2. **Discuss** the arguments for and against outsourcing and subcontracting, compared with provisions made by the firm.

© The IBO, 2007

Make or buy decisions
(HIGHER LEVEL FOCUS)

Make or buy decisions are concerned with whether or not a firm should produce a product or purchase it from another firm. Make or buy decisions involve both qualitative and quantitative considerations.

Quantitative considerations

√ Investment appraisals

√ Cost-benefit analysis

√ Contribution/Marginal costing

√ Break-even analysis

Qualitative considerations

√ Product quality

√ Availability of technical expertise

√ Availability of labour

√ Level of demand for the product

√ Reliability of suppliers

√ Core competency of product or service

Make or buy example using contribution analysis

Caribbean Traders Ltd. manufactures chairs. At a production level of 20,000 units, the cost per unit is given below:

Materials	$10.00
Labour	$ 5.00
Other variable costs	$ 4.00
Fixed costs	$ 5.50
Total Cost	$24.50

The chairs, however, can be bought from another manufacturer for $20.00 per unit. Considering the costs presented here, should Caribbean Traders Ltd. make or buy the 20,000 chairs?

Answer

A decision can be made based on the following quantitative and qualitative considerations:

1. Given the marginal cost of $19.00 to manufacture one chair, when compared with the purchase price of $20.00, Caribbean Traders Ltd. must consider making the chairs.

2. The company must bear the fixed costs even if it decides to purchase the chairs.

3. The company stands to lose profit if it decides to purchase the chairs.

   That is, ($20.00 - $19.00) x 20,000= $ 20,000.

4. A decision to buy chairs results in idle capacity in the factory, e.g., machinery may be idle.

5. A decision to buy chairs also affects the company's employees: Some would be idle or have to be laid off.

You must be able to make appropriate **calculations** to support a decision to make or buy. © The IBO, 2007

5.8: PROJECT MANAGEMENT
(HIGHER LEVEL FOCUS)

Project management relates to the well-planned organisation and execution of action, processes and procedures towards the completion of a project, e.g., building a school. A number of tools are often used to ensure the successful completion of a project, and one such tool is **network analysis**.

Network analysis: This is used for planning and controlling the progress of projects. The Critical Path Analysis (CPA) is a network analysis which is frequently used to schedule and manage projects. More specifically, the Critical Path Analysis is used for the following purposes:

1. To estimate the earliest/latest start and end time for a particular task in a project

2. To estimate the minimum time required for completing the whole project

3. To identify the tasks which may be delayed and the ones which are critical to the project's completion

4. To identify cases where resources are not being used effectively

5. To continuously evaluate the success or failure of the planning and implementation process

6. To assist decision making.

Critical Path Analysis (CPA): The Process

The following elements are important for an effective Critical Path Analysis.

1. The project must be broken down into specific activities.

2. Each activity is sequenced based on its importance, relevance and support to other activities.

3. Each activity is assigned a duration from which the Earliest Start Times and Latest Finish Times can be determined.

4. The network is drawn.

5. The Earliest Start Time (EST) refers to the earliest time an activity can start. EST depends on the duration of preceding activities.

(Contd...)

6. Latest Finish Time (LFT) refers to the latest time by which an activity can finish. LFT is crucial to the completion of the entire project within a minimum timeframe.

7. Determine the **Critical Path**: The sequence of activities which determines the least time in which the project can be completed.

8. **Nodes** represent the start and finish of an activity.

9. **Arrows** represent the duration of an activity

10. **Total Float** represents the amount of time by which an activity can be delayed without extending the duration of the project. **Total Float = LFT – Duration - EST of an activity within the project.**

11. **Free Float** represents the time by which an activity can be delayed without affecting the start of the next activity. **Free Float = EST at the end – Duration – EST at the start.**

Critical Path Analysis: The process

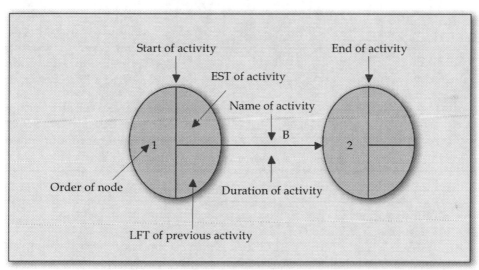

Example: A project is represented by the following information:

Activity	Preceding activity	Duration (in days)
A	None	6
B	None	3
C	None	2
D	C	2
E	B	1
F	D	1

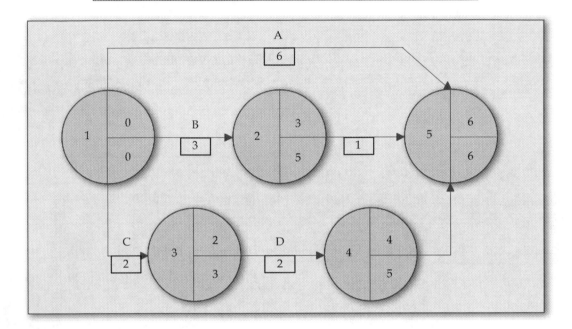

Interpretation of the network

The Earliest Start Times (EST)

1. From node # 1 we can see that activities A, B and C are carried out simultaneously and their Earliest Start Time is 0. The duration of each activity is 6, 3 and 2 days respectively.

2. From node # 2, activity B is followed by activity E. The Earliest Start Time for activity E is 3 days because it cannot begin until activity B has been completed. Note that the duration of activity E is 1 day.

3. From node # 3, activity D succeeds activity C. The earliest time activity D can start is 2 days because the duration of the preceding activity C is 2 days.

4. From node # 4, the Earliest Start Time for activity F is 4 days because activities C and D must be completed first.

5. From node #5, it can be seen that the total duration of the project is 6 days, which is the duration of activity A.

1. The project is to be completed in 6 days. This means that activity A must be completed in 6 days.

2. The Latest Finish Time of activity E is 5 days. This is calculated by subtracting the duration of activity E from Latest Finish Time at node #5.

3. The Latest Finish Times for all other activities are calculated in the same manner working from left to right throughout the network.

Pay careful attention to situations such as the example presented below

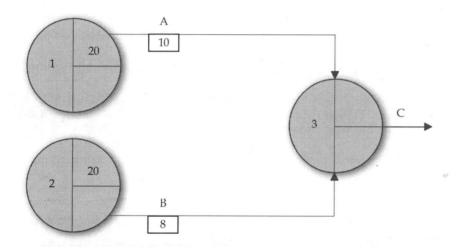

Given this situation where activities A and B are connected to one node, what is the EST of activity C?

1. Activity A   20 + 10 = 30

2. Activity B   20 + 8 = 28

Activity C cannot start until both activities A and B are completed. Given the duration of activity A (10 days), the earliest time activity C can start is 30 days after commencement.

Activity	Duration (days)	EST	LFT	Free Float	Total Float
A	6	0	6	0	0
B	3	0	2	0	2
C	2	0	1	0	1
D	2	2	3	0	1
E	1	3	5	2	2
F	1	4	5	1	1

(Contd...)

1. The **Free Float** represents the time by which an activity can be delayed without affecting the Earliest Start Time (EST) of the succeeding activity. From the table we can see that activity E can be delayed by 2 days while activity F can be delayed by 1 day.

2. The **Total Float** represents the amount of time by which an activity can be delayed without delaying the completion date of the project.

3. The **Critical Path** represents those activities which must be completed on time. These activities have no buffer time and if they are delayed, the duration of the whole project will be affected. Project delays can lead to a number of set backs for the firm, e.g., higher costs and loss of revenue.

4. **A note on Dummy activities:** A dummy activity is not a real activity; hence, it does not use up any resources. In some networks, dummy activities are used to depict the logical dependence between activities.

You must be able to **construct** and **interpret** a network, identify the critical path and calculate the free and total floats.

© The IBO, 2007

Project management: The value of networks

√ Help identify tasks which are critical to the completion of the project

√ Help determine the minimum time in which a project can be completed

√ Help identify possible delays in the activities or the whole project and take corrective action where necessary

√ Facilitate effective allocation and control of resources throughout the duration of the project

√ Help determine if an activity is interdependent or independent

√ Enhance project efficiency and facilitate project-cost management

---

Limitations of networks

√ Constructing networks, even with the use of the most sophisticated technology, is a timeconsuming and labour-intensive activity.

√ Networks do not factor in unforeseen qualitative factors, e.g., industrial action which may be taken by employees in the event of a dispute.

√ The complexity of networks adds to the challenges associated with their implementation.

√ Networks are limited to the scheduling of activities associated with large, complex projects.

You must be able to **evaluate** the value of a network in the management of a project.

© The IBO, 2007

What is business strategy?

Business strategy refers to action plans formulated in response to, or in anticipation of changes in the internal or external environment. Business strategy also focuses on achieving one or more long-term objectives.

The strategy-formulation process

When formulating business strategy, the management must consider the following factors which are crucial to the strategic planning process.

1. **The business's current position:**   Where is the business now?

2. **The business's future position:**   Where should the business be after a certain period?

3. **The action to be taken:**   What should be done to attain the future position?

Strategic Management

Strategic analysis
Analysing how the changes in external environment will influence the organisation's current and future positions and formulating possible responses which should be adopted. Strategic analysis involves the use of a combination of tools, such as Five Forces, SWOT and PEST.

Strategic choice
Strategic choice is about selecting the best strategy from a number of available strategic options. The focus is on selecting the most effective strategy that will enable the organisation to attain the future position.

Strategic implementation
Strategic implementation is about putting the chosen strategy into action.

NOTE:

The topic on strategy "does not add new content to the Diploma Programme Business and Management course but gathers together and synthesises business concepts and techniques from the topics in the HL course".

© The IBO, 2007

For an outline of the concepts and techniques associated with each stage of the strategic-management framework, refer to pages 40-42 of the International Baccalaureate Business and Management Diploma Programme guide, 2007.

INDEX